Two-Block Theme Quilts

Two-Block Theme Quilts

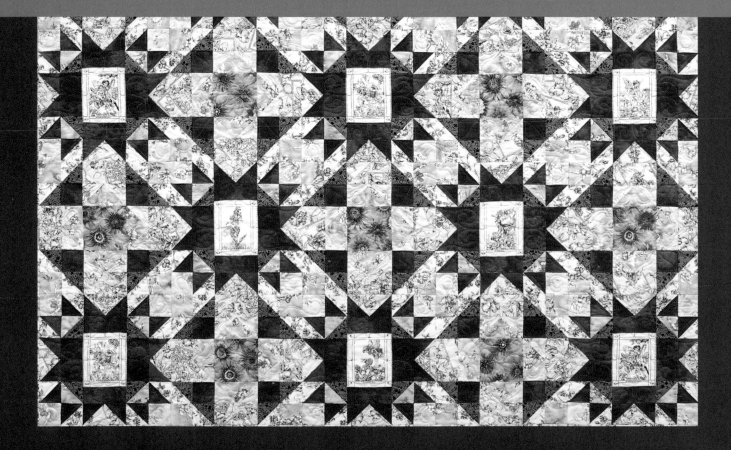

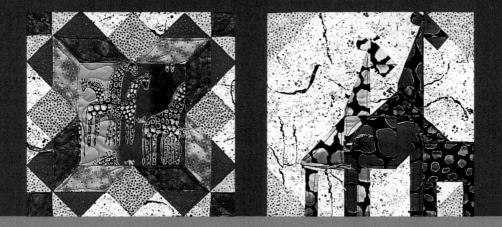

Claudia Olson

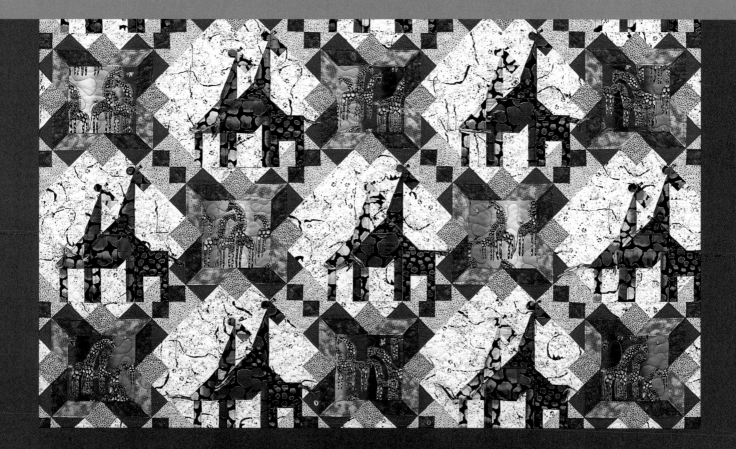

Two-Block Theme Quilts
© 2006 by Claudia Olson

Martingale ®
& COMPANY

That
Patchwork
Place®

That Patchwork Place® is an imprint of
Martingale & Company®.

Martingale & Company
20205 144th Avenue NE
Woodinville, WA 98072-8478 USA
www.martingale-pub.com

Credits

President: Nancy J. Martin

CEO: Daniel J. Martin

VP and General Manager: Tom Wierzbicki

Publisher: Jane Hamada

Editorial Director: Mary V. Green

Managing Editor: Tina Cook

Technical Editor: Ellen Pahl

Copy Editor: Sheila Chapman Ryan

Design Director: Stan Green

Illustrator: Robin Strobel

Cover and Text Designer: Stan Green

Photographer: Brent Kane

Printed in China
11 10 09 08 07 06   8 7 6 5 4 3 2 1

Library of Congress Cataloging-in-Publication Data

Olson, Claudia.
   Two-block theme quilts / Claudia Olson.
   ISBN 1-56477-654-9 (alk. paper)
   1. Patchwork—Patterns. 2. Quilting—Patterns. I. Title.
   TT835.O53 2005
   746.46'041—dc22

2005023700

Mission Statement
Dedicated to providing quality products and
service to inspire creativity.

Dedication

To my children, Andrea and Kelson.

Acknowledgments

I'd like to express great and sincere thanks to my quilting friends who kept deadlines and were willing to work hard for the creation of this book. They are Pat Peyton, Linda Krueger, Sandy Ashbrook, Marie Tiedemann, Dianne Gillin, Patty Stith, Sande Tennant, Stacey Mitchell, and Jane Wheeler. A special thank-you to Trudee Barritt, who worked late into the night to help me complete extra projects. Thanks also to Jill Therriault, Sandy Ashbrook, Linda Krueger, and Lynn Pittsinger, who willingly machine quilted the quilts.

Also, I would like to thank my editors, Sheila Ryan, Tina Cook, and Ellen Pahl, as well as the photographer, illustrator, and publisher, for their cooperative teamwork on this book. They were great to work with and have been fun people to get to know.

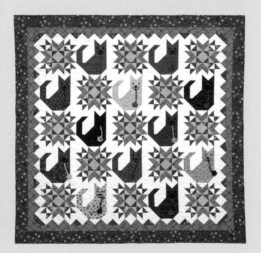

Contents

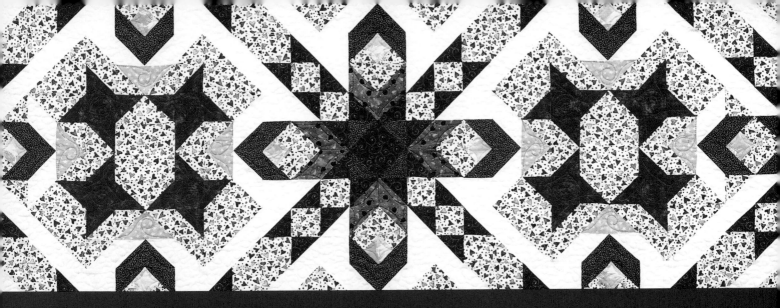

Introduction

When I set out to make quilts for my children, I had trouble finding patterns that would suit older children. Most of the patterns I found were designed for small children or babies, and had juvenile themes. So, I set to work designing quilts that would be suitable for older children. As always, I found myself drawn to a visually interesting two-block format. The patterns I created are represented by the quilts in this book, which include pieced animal blocks and character prints. I tried to keep the quilts whimsical, but also sophisticated enough for adults. When you look through this book, I hope that you find quilt patterns that interest both you and your family, young and old alike.

Choosing Color, Pattern, and Fabric

Each quilt in this book incorporates two blocks that work well together when placed side by side. When choosing a pattern to make, feel free to use the same colors as I did, or change them to suit yourself or the quilt recipient. Simply note the values of the fabrics used—the range of colors from light to dark. It's important to keep the fabric values similar to the pictured quilt if you want to see the primary and secondary designs appear in the same way.

If you select fabric with a character or conversation print, be sure that the designs printed on the fabric will fit into the space allotted in the pattern. Make a window template of the finished size of the fabric piece and use it to audition your fabric. For example, if the cutting instructions call for a 4½" square, cut a 4" square out of a piece of paper and place the paper over the prospective fabric. Look through the hole to see whether the print will fit.

Decide in advance if you want to fussy cut your pieces or cut pieces from straight strips. Cutting strips is easier, but you'll likely cut through the characters printed on the fabric and not show the whole shape. To fussy cut, cut through one layer of fabric by placing your rotary ruler directly over the design you want to cut around. Then carefully cut out the required piece, leaving a ¼" seam allowance on each side. Fussy cutting requires extra fabric, takes more time, and produces more waste, but the results are well worth the effort.

Lastly, consider for whom the quilt is intended and the recipient's tastes. Quilts are expressions from the heart of the quilter. We love the people we make quilts for and try to choose designs and fabrics that they will love. The quilts in this book cover a wide range of subjects. No matter whom you have in mind, I'm sure that you'll find the perfect quilt.

Fabric Essentials

Be sure to select 100%-cotton fabric. Usually quilting fabric is 42" wide, and the fabric requirements in this book are based upon that width.

Wash, dry, and press your fabric before cutting to eliminate any chance of shrinking in the final quilt.

Basic Quiltmaking Techniques

Read the following sections to become familiar with the cutting and piecing techniques used throughout this book.

Half-Square Triangles

Half-square triangles consist of two triangles sewn together to make a pieced square, often called a triangle square. Here's a shortcut method to use when you need to make a lot of triangle squares.

1. Layer two same-sized squares with right sides together. Draw a diagonal pencil line from corner to corner on the wrong side of the lighter-colored square.

2. Sew a scant ¼" from each side of the drawn line.

3. Cut on the drawn line to separate the two identical units. Press the seam allowances toward the darker fabric (unless instructed otherwise in your project directions).

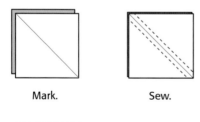

Mark. Sew.

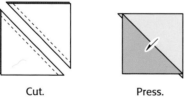

Cut. Press.

Quarter-Square Triangles

I like to use this method for making quarter-square triangles when the triangles always appear in the same position in a block. For instance, if the dark triangle will always be to the left of the light triangle,

Rotary Cutting Odd Measurements

Some of the quilts in this book call for cutting dimensions in measurements of ¹/₁₆". To cut ¹/₁₆", align your rotary ruler halfway between two ¹/₈" marks. Every ¹/₈" is equal to ²/₁₆", so if the cutting directions call for cutting ³/₁₆", align your ruler exactly halfway between the ¹/₄" line and the ³/₈" line. For ¹⁵/₁₆", use the halfway point between ⁷/₈" and 1" on your ruler, and so on.

or vice versa, then this shortcut method for sewing the units will ensure that you don't stitch triangles into the wrong position.

1. Layer two squares with right sides together and draw intersecting lines from corner to corner.

2. Stitch a scant ¼" from one side of each drawn line as shown, and stop stitching where the lines intersect. As you rotate the squares to stitch each subsequent seam, make sure that you're always sewing on the same side of the marked line (either always on the right or always on the left). The instructions for each project will tell you whether to stitch on the left or right side of the lines.

3. Cut along the drawn lines and press the seams.

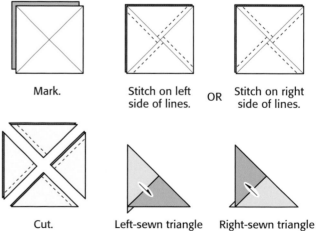

Mark.   Stitch on left side of lines. OR Stitch on right side of lines.

Cut.   Left-sewn triangle   Right-sewn triangle

Press.

Quick Corner Triangles

Quick corner triangles are made by sewing squares to the corners of larger squares or rectangles.

1. Using a pencil and ruler, draw a diagonal line on the wrong side of the smaller square.

2. With right sides together, pin this square to the corner of the larger piece as called for in your project directions. Sew on the drawn line.

3. Flip open the new corner triangle over the existing corner and press. If the triangle reaches the fabric edges of the underneath piece, trim the seam to ¼" from the drawn line. If the edges don't align, resew the seam and press again before trimming.

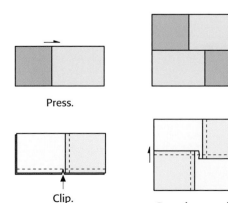

Stitch on marked line,
trim, and press.

Triangle-Trio Squares

I learned the following method for making Shaded Four Patch blocks from Sally Schneider's book *Scrap Frenzy*. She named it Mary's Triangles, for her friend Mary. I call it triangle-trio squares because the piecing produces one large and two small triangles in a pieced square. This example shows a simple square in the corner, but some pattern directions substitute a triangle square. This method produces two triangle-trio squares.

1. Sew a rectangle to a small square, right sides together. Repeat to make a second unit. Sew these units together along their long edges, positioning the small squares in opposite corners. Turn the unit to the wrong side and snip the seam allowance all the way to the seam at the halfway point. Press the seam in two directions, away from the small squares.

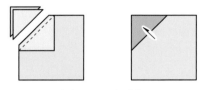

Press.

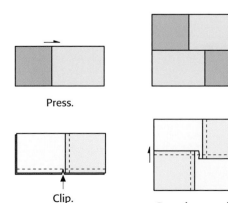

Clip.

Press in opposing
directions.

2. Make a triangle template from either cardboard or template plastic. To do so, draw a square as specified in the project instructions, and then draw a diagonal line on the square. Cut on the line to make the triangle template.

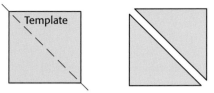

Template

3. Place the triangle template on one corner of the unit's wrong side, positioning the 90° corner over one of the small squares as shown. Draw a diagonal line along the template edge. The drawn line should intersect the corner of the small square's seam allowance. Draw a second line with the template placed on the opposite corner.

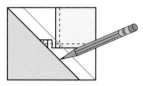

4. Position the sewn unit over an unpieced rectangle, right sides together, and sew them together on each drawn line. Cut diagonally, halfway between the sewn lines. Don't be alarmed that your seam allowance is larger than ¼"; you can trim it if desired. Press the seam allowances toward the large triangles.

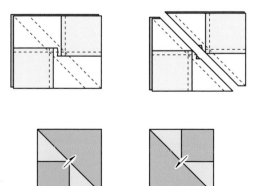

Flying-Geese Units

The following method makes it easy to make several flying-geese units at once, and it's extremely accurate. One sewn unit produces four flying-geese units.

1. Using a pencil and ruler, draw a diagonal line on the wrong side of four small squares. Position two of them on opposite corners of a large square, right sides together and overlapping at the inner corners. Sew a scant ¼" on each side of the drawn line. Cut the unit apart on the drawn line. Press the seam allowances toward the small triangles.

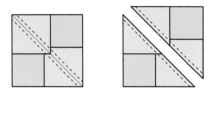

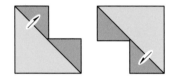

2. Position the remaining small squares on the corners of the large triangles, right sides together, aligning the drawn lines as shown. Sew a scant ¼" on each side of the drawn line. Cut apart on the drawn line. Press the seam allowances toward the small triangles. You'll now have four perfectly sewn flying-geese units.

Paper Foundation Piecing

Some of the patterns in this book use paper foundation piecing. This is helpful when the piece is an odd shape.

1. To make a paper foundation, photocopy or trace the pattern from the book. Then place the pattern on a light table or windowpane. The light that shines through the glass will allow you to trace the lines onto the back side of your paper.

2. After tracing the lines on the back side of the paper, position fabric piece 1 right side up, over the space indicated on the right side of the pattern, being sure to allow for a ¼" seam to overlap the lines, and pin it in place.

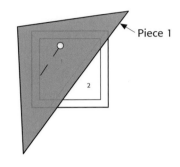

Piece 1

3. Place piece 2 over piece 1, right sides together, aligning the raw edges. Pin piece 2 in place, pinning through both layers of fabric and the paper. Remove or adjust the pin in piece 1 as needed.

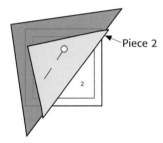

Piece 2

4. Turn the paper over and sew along the drawn line that is the seam line between pieces 1 and 2. Use a smaller than normal stitch length; this will help you tear away the paper later without pulling out stitches.

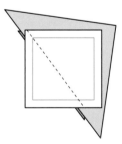

5. Unpin and fold piece 2 over into position and press.

6. When all the pieces are sewn in place, trim the outer edges, leaving a ¼" seam allowance. Crinkle the paper and remove it by tearing along the sewn lines.

Embellishing

Embellishing your finished blocks with embroidery or special quilting can give your quilts definition, detail, and interest. Look through the quilt photographs and patterns to see how the creatures and characters were given personality through embellishments. Add eyes, whiskers, expressions, or frills using the popular stitches shown below.

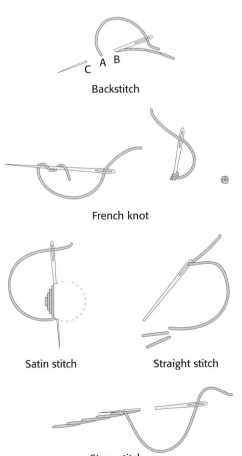

Backstitch

French knot

Satin stitch   Straight stitch

Stem stitch

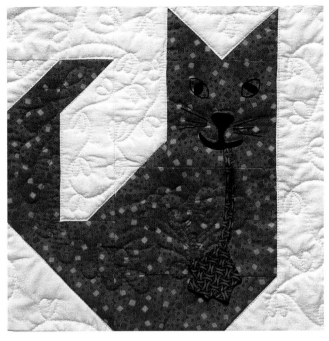

Embroidery detail from "Wyoming Alley Cats" quilt

Embroidery detail from "Albany Giraffes" quilt

Adding Borders

Most of the quilts in this book include one of two different types of borders: pieced borders and strip borders. Use the following methods for best results when adding borders.

Strip Borders

Strip borders are plain borders made of long pieces of fabric. I cut strip borders on the lengthwise grain, but this often requires more fabric. The projects include yardage amounts for borders cut either crosswise or lengthwise.

> ALERT: If you want to cut lengthwise border strips, you *must* cut them first, before cutting any other pieces from the fabric. The remaining fabric will be narrower and will require cutting more strips than indicated in the cutting charts.

Border strips cut crosswise must sometimes be pieced to achieve the necessary length. To piece strips, join them with a 45° or 60° angle to achieve a pleasing appearance. Strip borders can be finished with squared corners or with mitered corners. Instructions for each method are given below.

Squared Corners

1. Measure the quilt top through the center to get an accurate measurement. Cut or piece the side border strips to this length.

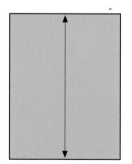

Measure vertical center.

2. Mark with pins the half and quarter points on the side border strips and quilt top. Match the pins and pin the borders to the quilt top. Sew; press the seam allowances toward the borders. Measure the quilt top horizontally through the center. Cut or piece the top and botom border strips to this measurement and sew them to the quilt top.

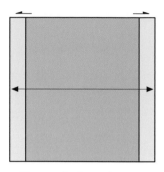

Measure horizontal center.

Mitered Corners

1. Measure the length of the quilt top vertically through the center. Add two times the width of your border plus 4" to this measurement; this will be the length to cut the side border strips. Measure the width of the quilt through the center and add the same amount; this will be the length to cut the top and bottom borders.

2. Fold the quilt top in half and then in fourths and place pins at these points.

3. Mark the length of the quilt (centered) onto the two side border strips using straight pins. Then fold each border strip in half, aligning the two pins, to find the midpoint of the border. Mark the midpoint, and then fold in half again to mark the border in fourths. With right sides together, pin the border strips to the sides of the quilt top, matching the pins.

4. Sew the borders to the sides of the quilt top, stopping and starting ¼" from the pin at each end and backstitching to secure the seam. Press seams toward the borders.

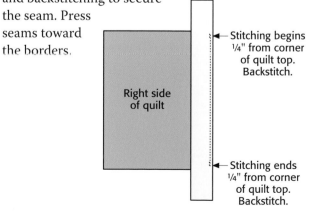

Right side of quilt

Stitching begins ¼" from corner of quilt top. Backstitch.

Stitching ends ¼" from corner of quilt top. Backstitch.

5. For the top and bottom borders, measure and mark the end points as well as the midpoint and quarter points on the borders and quilt top. Pin the borders in place and stitch as before, starting and stopping ¼" from each end of the quilt top. Note that the border strips will extend beyond each end of the quilt and overlap the side borders. Press the seam allowances toward the borders.

6. To create the miters, work with the quilt right side up and lay one strip on top of the adjacent border. Fold the top border under at a 45° angle so that it aligns with the adjacent border. Press and pin the fold in place.

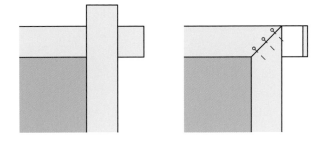

7. Position a 90°-triangle ruler or Bias Square® ruler over the corner to check that the corner is flat and square. Unpin the crease, adjust, if necessary, and re-press the fold firmly to create a crease.

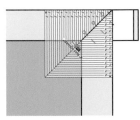

8. Fold the center section of the quilt top diagonally from the corner so the right sides are together, aligning the long edges of the borders. On the wrong side, draw a pencil line along the diagonal crease of the border and position the pins on both sides of the drawn line.

9. Beginning at the inside corner, backstitch and then stitch along the drawn line toward the outside point, being careful not to stitch into the quilt top or to stretch the fabric. Backstitch at the end of the seam. Turn the quilt top over and check the mitered corner. If the corner is acceptable, turn the quilt to the back

and trim the excess border fabric to a ¼" seam allowance. Press the seam allowances to one side. Repeat to complete all four corners.

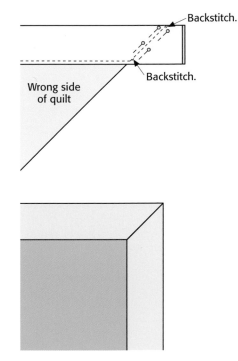

Completed miter

Finishing the Quilt

Now your quilt is ready for the finishing steps of layering, basting, quilting, and binding.

Layering and Basting

Press the entire quilt top carefully and snip any long or raveling threads. With the wrong side of the backing up, layer the batting on top of the backing. Place the quilt top, right side up, on the batting. Smooth out all layers, creating a wrinkle-free surface.

For hand quilting, baste the layers together with cotton basting thread in horizontal and vertical rows approximately 6" to 8" apart. For machine quilting, use safety pins spaced 4" to 6" apart for holding the layers together.

Machine or hand quilt as desired.

Batting Tip: You can eliminate wrinkles in your batting by tumbling it in the dryer for 5 to 10 minutes on air only, no heat.

Binding

1. Sew the 2¼" binding strips together end to end with 45° or 60° diagonal seams to make one continuous strip. Cut the beginning end of the strip at the same angle and press under ¼". Fold the pieced strip lengthwise, wrong sides together, and press.

2. Matching raw edges, place the beginning of the binding about halfway down one side of the front of the quilt. Begin stitching about 3" from the beginning of the binding, taking a few backstitches and using a scant ¼" seam allowance. Leave the beginning 3" unstitched for now.

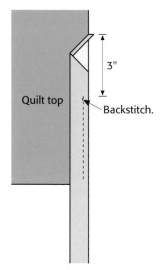

3. Stop ¼" from the corner of the quilt and, with the needle still in the fabric, pivot the quilt 45° and stitch to the outer corner of the quilt; backstitch.

4. Lift the needle and remove the quilt from the machine. Fold the binding strip up and away from the quilt at a 45° angle; then fold it back down, even with the edge of the quilt. Begin sewing at the folded edge and sew to ¼" from the next corner.

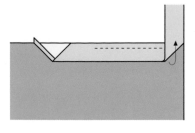

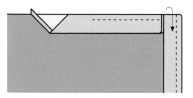

5. Repeat steps 3 and 4 at each corner. Stop sewing 3" from where you began, backstitch, and remove the quilt from the machine. Trim the binding end at an angle, leaving enough fabric to tuck into the folded beginning tail.

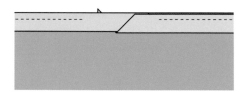

6. Tuck the ending tail into the beginning tail, pin, and finish sewing the binding to the quilt. Turn the folded edge to the back of the quilt and hand stitch it in place.

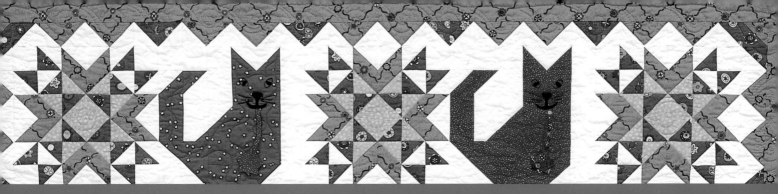

Quilts with Character Blocks

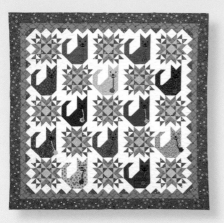

Wyoming Alley Cats

Page 18

Paper Doll Trade

Page 26

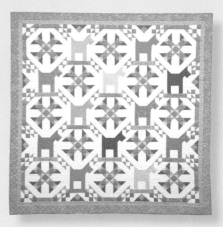

Star of the Dog Show

Page 34

Alaskan Ducks

Page 42

Albany Giraffes

Page 50

Wyoming Alley Cats

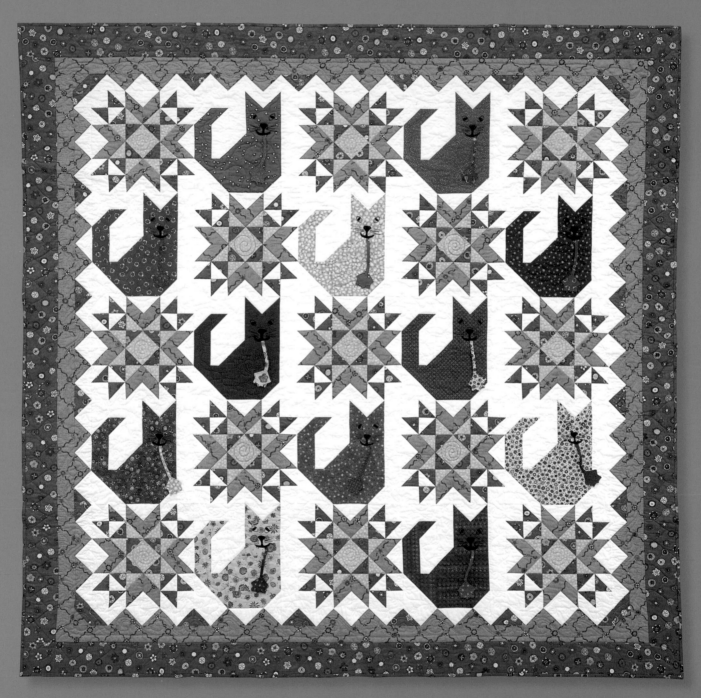

Designed by Claudia Olson and made by Jane Wheeler. Machine quilted by Lynn Pittsinger.
Finished quilt: 76" x 76" » Finished blocks: 12"

This whimsical quilt features cats with mice caught by their tails. Each cat and mouse is made from a different fabric—a fun way to use up your bright fat quarters. Use your favorite vivid colors or cat-inspired prints in this quilt that's perfect for the cat lover in your life.

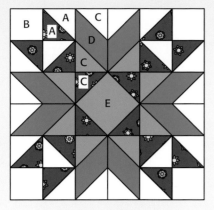

Wyoming Valley block

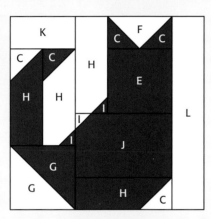

Alley Cat block

Materials

Yardage is based on 42"-wide fabric.

- 3¼ yards of white print for Wyoming Valley blocks, Alley Cat blocks, and pieced border
- 2⅝ yards of royal blue print for Wyoming Valley blocks, borders, and binding*
- 2 yards of green print for Wyoming Valley blocks and borders*
- ⅞ yard of turquoise print for Wyoming Valley blocks
- ¾ yard of blue print or 1 fat quarter *each* of 3 different blue prints for Alley Cat blocks and mice
- ¾ yard of purple print or 1 fat quarter *each* of 3 different purple prints for Alley Cat blocks and mice
- ¾ yard of hot pink print or 1 fat quarter *each* of 3 different hot pink prints for Alley Cat blocks and mice
- ¾ yard of yellow print or 1 fat quarter *each* of 3 different yellow prints for Alley Cat blocks and mice
- ⅛ yard of black print or scraps for Alley Cat blocks (appliquéd nose-and-mouth units)
- 4⅝ yards of fabric for backing
- 82" x 82" piece of batting
- Embroidery floss in black, green, gold, and blue
- ¼" bias press bar

If you prefer to cut lengthwise borders, you'll need 2⅞ yards of royal blue print and 2¼ yards of green print.

CUTTING FOR 13 WYOMING VALLEY BLOCKS

Fabric	Piece	Number of Strips	Strip Width	Cut
White	A	6	2⅞"	78 squares, 2⅞" x 2⅞"
	B	4	2½"	52 squares, 2½" x 2½"
	C	6 and remainder of B strip	2½"	104 squares, 2½" x 2½"
Royal Blue	A	6	2⅞"	78 squares, 2⅞" x 2⅞"
	C	4	2½"	52 squares, 2½" x 2½"
Green	D	7	4½"	104 rectangles, 2½" x 4½"
Turquoise	C	7	2½"	104 squares, 2½" x 2½"
	E	2	4½"	13 squares, 4½" x 4½"

Piecing the Wyoming Valley Blocks

1. Referring to "Half-Square Triangles" on page 10, layer a white A square on a royal blue A square. Stitch, cut, and press. Repeat with all 78 squares to make 156 triangle squares.

Make 156.

2. Sew three triangle squares together with one white B square as shown. Make 52.

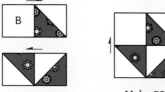

Make 52.

3. Referring to "Quick Corner Triangles" on page 11, sew a white C square to one corner of a green D rectangle. Sew a turquoise C square to the opposite corner as shown. Make 52 of each mirror image.

Make 52 of each.

4. Sew the mirror-image units from step 3 together in pairs, press, and trim. Make 52.

Make 52.

5. Use the quick-corner-triangle technique to sew royal blue C squares to each corner of a turquoise E square. Press and trim. Make 13.

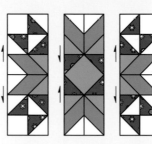 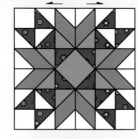

Make 13.

6. Lay out the pieced units from steps 2–5 as shown. Sew the units together into rows. Join the rows to complete a Wyoming Valley block. Make 13.

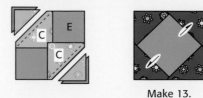

Make 13.

Piecing the Alley Cat Blocks

1. Use the quick-corner-triangle technique to sew a purple C square on one corner of a white F rectangle. Stitch, cut, and press. Repeat on the opposite corner.

2. Using the half-square-triangle method, position a white G square on a purple G square. Stitch, cut, and press. You'll have two triangle squares. Set one aside for another block if you are using yardage. If you are using fat quarters, one will be extra.

CUTTING FOR 12 ALLEY CAT BLOCKS

Fabric	Piece	Number of Strips	Strip Width	Cut	
				Yardage	**12 Fat Quarters**
Blue, Purple, Hot Pink, and Yellow	C	1 of each color	2½"	9 squares, 2½" x 2½", of each color	3 squares per fat quarter
	G	1 of each color	4⅞"	2 squares, 4⅞" x 4⅞", of each color	1 square per fat quarter
	H	1 of each color	2½"	6 rectangles, 2½" x 6½", of each color	2 squares per fat quarter
	I	1 of each color	1½"	6 squares, 1½" x 1½", of each color	2 squares per fat quarter
	E	1 of each color	4½"	3 squares, 4½" x 4½", of each color	1 square per fat quarter
	J	Remainder of matching E strip	4½"	3 rectangles, 4½" x 6½", of each color	1 square per fat quarter
White	C	2	2½"	24 squares, 2½" x 2½"	
	F	1	4½"	12 rectangles, 2½" x 4½"	
	G	1	4⅞"	8 squares, 4⅞" x 4⅞"*	
	H	4	2½"	24 rectangles, 2½" x 6½"	
	I	1	1½"	12 squares, 1½" x 1½"	
	K	1	4½"	12 rectangles, 2½" x 4½"	
	L	4	2½"	12 rectangles, 2½" x 12½"	
Black	Nose-and-mouth units	Cut 12 nose-and-mouth appliqué shapes using the pattern on page 25.			

If you are using fat quarters, cut 12 white G squares to have 1 for each fat quarter.

3. Using the quick-corner-triangle technique, place white C squares on two purple H rectangles as shown. Sew, press, and trim to make one of each mirror image.

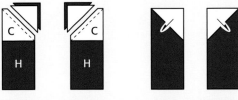

Make 1 of each.

4. Sew purple I squares to the lower-right corners of two white H rectangles. Sew a purple C square to the upper-left corner of *one* of the white H rectangles.

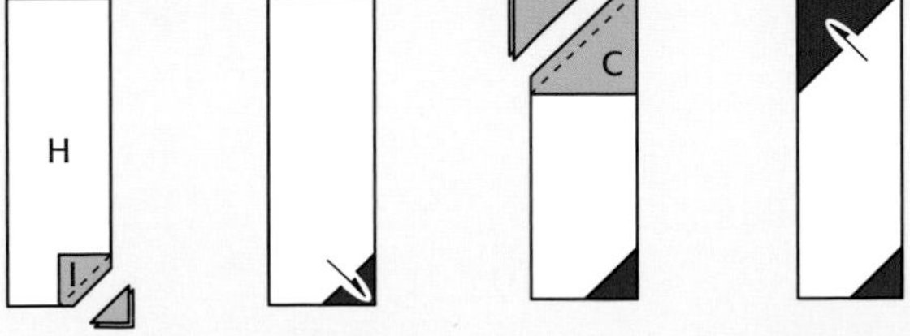

Make 2.

From the 2, make 1.

5. Sew a white I square to the upper-left corner of a purple J rectangle as shown.

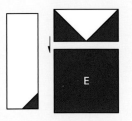

6. Sew the flying-geese unit made in step 1 to the top of a purple E square to complete the cat's head. Then add the white H rectangle with the purple I triangle (made in step 4) to the left side of the cat's head.

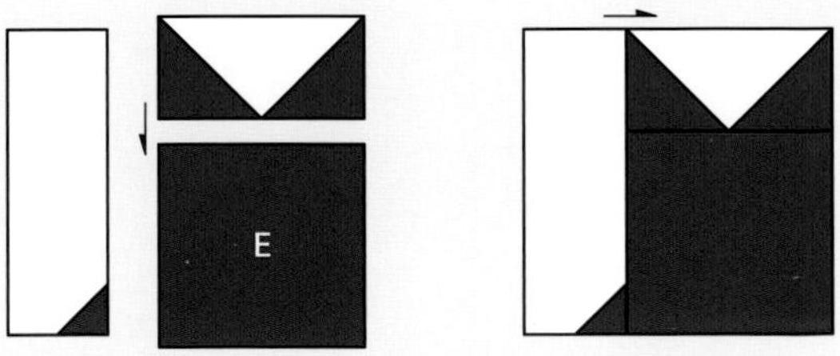

7. Lay out the cat's-head unit, the pieced purple J rectangle, and a pieced purple H rectangle as shown; sew them together.

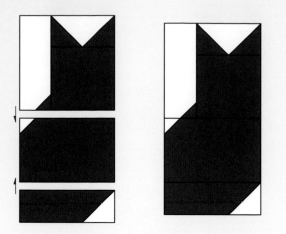

8. Lay out a white K rectangle, a pieced white H rectangle, a pieced purple H rectangle, and a G triangle square as shown; sew them together. Press.

K

9. Sew the rows made in steps 7 and 8 together. Add a white L rectangle to the right side of the cat to complete a purple Alley Cat block.

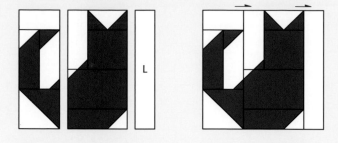

10. Repeat steps 1–9 to make a total of three purple, three blue, three hot pink, and three yellow Alley Cat blocks.

11. Referring to the eye placement diagram on page 25, embroider the outline of the cats' eyes using a stem stitch and two strands of black floss. Then use black, green, gold, or blue embroidery floss to stitch the iris with a satin stitch. Last, embroider the cats' whiskers with black embroidery floss using a backstitch.

CUTTING FOR 12 MICE					
Fabric	**Piece**	**Number of Strips from Each Fabric**	**Strip Width**	**Cut**	
				Yardage	**12 Fat Quarters**
Blue, Purple, Hot Pink, and Yellow	M (ears)	1	1⅜" x 15"	6 squares, 1⅜" x 1⅜", of each color	2 squares per fat quarter
	N (body)	1	2" x 15"	6 squares, 2" x 2", of each color	2 squares per fat quarter
	O (tail)	1 bias strip	1⅛" x 20"	3 bias strips, 1⅛" x 6", of each color	1 bias strip per fat quarter

Piecing the Mice

1. Sew two hot pink M squares right sides together. Cut the sewn squares once diagonally to make two ears. Trim the seams to ⅛". Turn the sewn ears right side out.

2. Embroider two French knot eyes on one hot pink N square, using two strands of black embroidery floss.

French knots

3. Sew the embroidered hot pink N square to a plain hot pink N square, right sides together, with the two ears placed on the inside as shown. Leave an opening at the corner opposite the ears to turn the square and to later insert the tail. Turn the sewn square right side out and press.

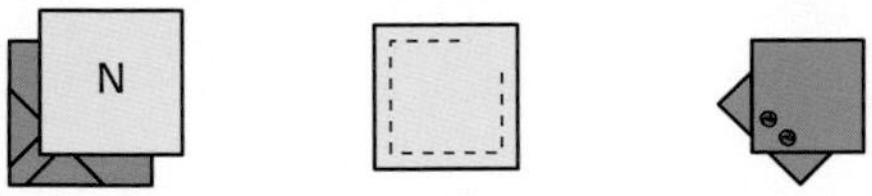

4. Make a tail by folding a hot pink O bias strip in half lengthwise, wrong sides together, and then sew with a ¼" seam. Trim the seam to ⅛". Insert a ¼" plastic or metal bias bar into the sewn tube and turn the seam to one side of the bar. Press the seam flat against the bias bar. Cut the bias-strip tail to be 4" long.

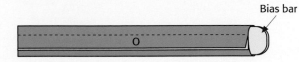

Bias bar

5. Insert the tail into the opening left in the mouse body. Topstitch around the edges of the mouse body, securing the tail.

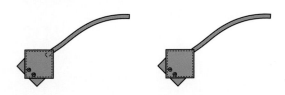

6. Repeat to make a total of 12 mice: three blue, three purple, three yellow, and three hot pink.

7. Appliqué the nose-and-mouth units onto the cats' faces, leaving an opening along the bottom edge of each mouth. Tuck the tails of the mice into the openings of the cats' mouths, being careful to turn the seams of the tails toward the quilt. Use a different-colored mouse with each cat. Sew the opening of the cats' mouths closed. The mice will hang loose.

Fabric	Piece	Number of Strips	Strip Width	First Cut	Second Cut
Green	P	2	5¼"	10 squares, 5¼" x 5¼"	Cut all squares ⊠
	A	Remainder of P strip	2⅞"	2 squares, 2⅞" x 2⅞"	
	Border	8	2½"		
White	P	1	5¼"	5 squares, 5¼" x 5¼"	Cut all squares ⊠
	A	3 and remainder of P strip	2⅞"	40 squares, 2⅞" x 2⅞"	Cut 20 squares ⊡
Royal Blue	A	2	2⅞"	22 squares, 2⅞" x 2⅞"	
	Border	8	4¼"		
	Binding	8	2¼"		

CUTTING FOR BORDERS AND BINDING

Making the Pieced Border

1. Sew a green P triangle on each end of a white P triangle as shown. Sew a white A triangle on each end. Make 20.

Make 20.

2. Using the half-square-triangle technique, place a white A square on a royal blue A square. Draw, stitch, cut, and press. Sew 20 to make 40 triangle squares. Repeat with a green A square on a royal blue A square. Sew two to make four triangle squares.

Make 40.   Make 4.

3. Sew a white/royal blue triangle square to each end of the unit made in step 1 to make a border section. Make 20.

Make 20.

4. Sew five border sections together end to end. Make four. Add a green/royal blue triangle square to each end of two of the pieced borders, making the royal blue triangle face inward.

Assembling the Quilt Top

1. Arrange the blocks in rows, alternating the blocks as shown. Sew the blocks into rows, pressing the seams in opposite direction from row to row. Join the rows.

2. Sew the two pieced borders without corner units to the sides of the quilt top. Sew the two pieced borders with corner units to the top and bottom edges of the quilt.

3. Sew the green 2½" border strips end to end to form one long strip. Refer to "Adding Borders" on page 14 to measure your quilt and cut border strips to fit. Add the green borders to the quilt.

4. Repeat step 3 with the royal blue 4¼" border strips.

Finishing the Quilt

Referring to "Finishing the Quilt" on page 15, prepare the backing fabric and then layer the backing, batting, and quilt top. After basting the layers together, hand or machine quilt as desired; then bind your quilt using the 2¼"-wide royal blue strips.

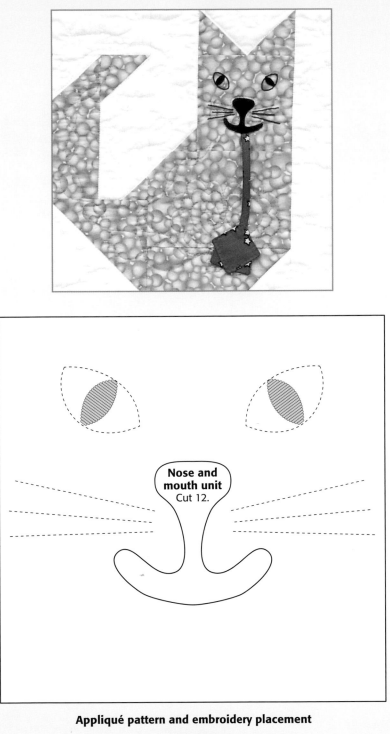

Appliqué pattern and embroidery placement

═══ Satin stitch

- - - - Backstitch

Paper Doll Trade

Designed by Claudia Olson and made by Marie Tiedeman. Machine quilted by Lynn Pittsinger.
Finished quilt: 50" x 50" » Finished blocks: 8"

Paper Doll blocks are paired with Free Trade blocks to make this colorful, fun quilt. Choose a variety of bright prints, or use fabrics from your child's outgrown clothing to make the dolls.

Free Trade block

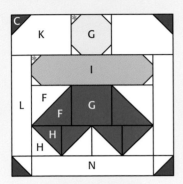

Boy Paper Doll block

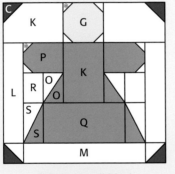

Girl Paper Doll block
* Indicates piece J

Materials

Yardage is based on 42"-wide fabric.

- 2 yards of white print for blocks and pieced border
- 1¾ yards of royal blue print for blocks, border, and binding*
- 1 yard of hot pink print for Free Trade blocks and border**
- ½ yard of yellow print for Free Trade blocks and pieced border
- ¼ yard of magenta print for Free Trade blocks
- ¼ yard of light pink print for Free Trade blocks
- ¼ yard *total* of green prints for Paper Doll blocks
- ⅜ yard *total* of blue prints for Paper Doll blocks
- ¼ yard *total* of bright pink prints for Paper Doll blocks
- ¼ yard *total* of yellow prints for Paper Doll blocks
- ⅛ yard of flesh-tone print for Paper Doll blocks
- Scraps of purple print and red print for Paper Doll blocks
- 3⅛ yards of fabric for backing
- 56" x 56" piece of batting

Includes enough yardage for borders to be cut lengthwise or crosswise.

**If you prefer to cut borders lengthwise, you'll need 1½ yards.*

CUTTING FOR 13 FREE TRADE BLOCKS				
Fabric	**Piece**	**Number of Strips**	**Strip Width**	**Cut**
Yellow	B	1	1⅞"	13 squares, 1⅞" x 1⅞"
	C	5	1½"	130 squares, 1½" x 1½"
Royal Blue	A	3	3¼"	26 squares, 3¼" x 3¼"
	B	4	1⅞"	65 squares, 1⅞" x 1⅞"
White	B	3	1⅞"	52 squares, 1⅞" x 1⅞"
	D	2	3¼"	13 squares, 3¼" x 3¼"
	E	2	5¼"	13 squares, 5¼" x 5¼"
Hot Pink	A	3	3¼"	26 squares, 3¼" x 3¼"
Magenta	B	3	1⅞"	52 squares, 1⅞" x 1⅞"
Light Pink	C	2	1½"	52 squares, 1½" x 1½"

Piecing the Free Trade Blocks

1. Referring to "Half-Square Triangles" on page 10, place a yellow B square on a royal blue B square. Stitch, cut, and press. Sew 13 to make 26 triangle squares. Repeat with 52 white B squares and 52 royal blue B squares to make 104 triangle squares.

Make 26. Make 104.

2. Sew the triangle squares to yellow C squares to form four-patch units as shown. Make 13 with yellow/blue triangle squares and 52 with white/blue triangle squares.

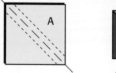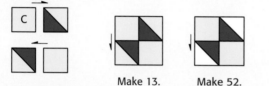

Make 13. Make 52.

3. Repeat the half-square-triangle technique with a hot pink A square and a royal blue A square. Sew 26 to make 52 triangle squares.

Make 52.

4. Referring to "Flying-Geese Units" on page 12, place triangle squares from step 3 on two corners of a white E square, with the blue triangles at the corner. Draw, sew, cut, and press. Sew another triangle square to the remaining white corners of the resulting units to make four flying-geese units as shown. Repeat with 12 more white E squares to create a total of 52 flying-geese units.

Make 52.

5. Repeat the flying-geese technique with magenta B squares and white D squares. Make 13 to create 52 flying-geese units.

Make 52.

6. Sew the magenta flying-geese units made in step 5 to opposite sides of a yellow/blue four-patch unit made in step 2 as shown. Make 13. Sew light pink C squares on opposite ends of the remaining magenta flying-geese units. Make 26.

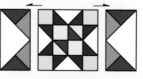

Make 13. Make 26.

7. Sew the units from step 6 together to make a center star. Make 13.

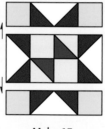

8. Sew flying-geese units made in step 4 to opposite sides of the center star made in step 7. Make 13. Then sew the remaining four-patch units from step 2 to opposite ends of 26 of the flying-geese units as shown.

Make 13.

Make 13. Make 26.

9. Join the units to complete the block. Make 13.

Make 13.

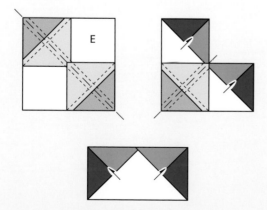

CUTTING FOR 12 PAPER DOLL BLOCKS

Fabric	Number of Strips	Strip Width	Piece	First Cut	Second Cut
White	2	1⅞"	B	12 squares, 1⅞" x 1⅞"	
			O	6 rectangles, 1⅞" x 2½"	Cut all rectangles 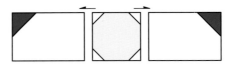
			S	6 rectangles, 1⅞" x 3¼"	Cut all rectangles
	1	2⅞"	F	6 squares, 2⅞" x 2⅞"	
	1	2⅜"	H	12 squares, 2⅜" x 2⅜"	
	4	1"	J	96 squares, 1" x 1"	
			M	6 rectangles, 1" x 6½"	
	2	3½"	K	24 rectangles, 2½" x 3½"	
	1	5½"	L	24 rectangles, 1½" x 5½"	
	2	1½"	N	6 rectangles, 1½" x 6½"	
			R	12 rectangles, 1½" x 2"	
Flesh Tone	1	2½"	G	12 squares, 2½" x 2½"	
Royal Blue	1	1⅞"	B	12 squares, 1⅞" x 1⅞"	
	1	1½"	C	24 squares, 1½" x 1½"	

Piecing the Paper Doll Blocks

1. Referring to "Quick Corner Triangles" on page 11, sew white J squares on the corners of a flesh tone G square. Make 12.

Make 12.

2. Use the same quick-corner-triangle method to sew a royal blue C square to one corner of a white K rectangle as shown. Make 12 of each mirror image.

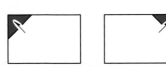

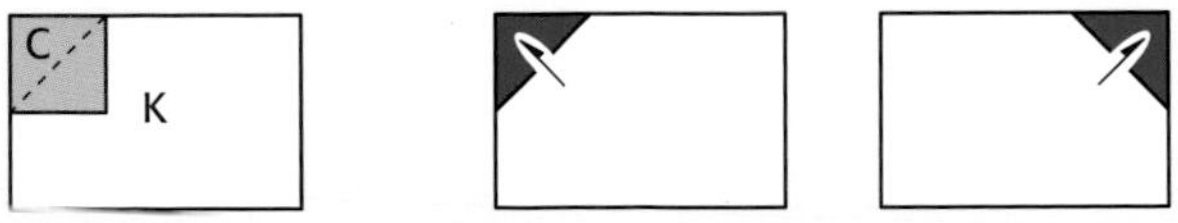

Make 12 of each.

3. Sew a unit from step 2 to each side of a unit from step 1 to make a head section as shown. Repeat to make 12.

4. Referring to "Half-Square Triangles" on page 10, layer a white B square on a royal blue B square. Draw, sew, cut, and press. Make 12 to create 24 triangle squares.

Make 24.

5. Sew a white L rectangle to the top of each unit from step 4 (along the white edges) as shown. Make 12 of each mirror image.

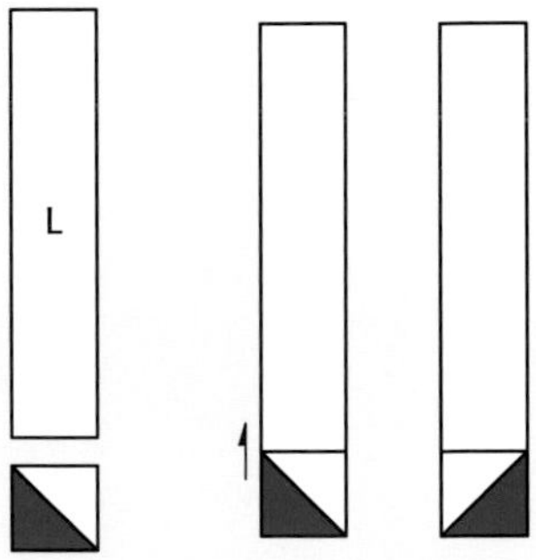

Make 12 of each.

CUTTING THE PAPER DOLL CLOTHES

Fabrics	Piece	First Cut	Second Cut
Blue Prints	F (pants)	5 squares, 2⅞" x 2⅞"	
	G (pants)	5 squares, 2½" x 2½"	
	H (pants)	10 squares, 2⅜" x 2⅜"	
	I (shirt)	2 rectangles, 2½" x 6½"	
	K (dress)	1 rectangle, 2½" x 3½"	
	O (dress)	1 rectangle, 1⅞" x 2½"	Cut rectangle ◻
	P (dress)	2 rectangles, 2" x 2½"	
	Q (dress)	1 rectangle, 2½" x 4½"	
	S (dress)	1 rectangle, 1⅞" x 3¼"	Cut rectangle ◻
Green Prints	F (pants)	1 square, 2⅞" x 2⅞"	
	G (pants)	1 square, 2½" x 2½"	
	H (pants)	2 squares, 2⅜" x 2⅜"	
	I (shirt)	2 rectangles, 2½" x 6½"	
	K (dress)	1 rectangle, 2½" x 3½"	
	O (dress)	1 rectangle, 1⅞" x 2½"	Cut rectangle ◻
	P (dress)	2 rectangles, 2" x 2½"	
	Q (dress)	1 rectangle, 2½" x 4½"	
	S (dress)	1 rectangle, 1⅞" x 3¼"	Cut rectangle ◻
Purple Print	I (shirt)	1 rectangle, 2½" x 6½"	
Red Print	I (shirt)	1 rectangle, 2½" x 6½"	
Bright Pinks	K (dress)	2 rectangles, 2½" x 3½"	
	O (dress)	2 rectangles, 1⅞" x 2½"	Cut all rectangles ◻
	P (dress)	4 rectangles, 2" x 2½"	
	Q (dress)	2 rectangles, 2½" x 4½"	
	S (dress)	2 rectangles, 1⅞" x 3¼"	Cut all rectangles ◻
Yellow Prints	K (dress)	2 rectangles, 2½" x 3½"	
	O (dress)	2 rectangles, 1⅞" x 2½"	Cut all rectangles ◻
	P (dress)	4 rectangles, 2" x 2½"	
	Q (dress)	2 rectangles, 2½" x 4½"	
	S (dress)	2 rectangles, 1⅞" x 3¼"	Cut all rectangles ◻

Piecing the Boy Paper Dolls

1. Using the half-square-triangle technique, place a white F square on a blue print F square. Draw, sew, cut, and press. Make one to create two triangle squares. Repeat with a white H square on a blue H square. Make two to create four triangle squares.

Make 2.   Make 4.

2. Sew the four H triangle squares together as shown.

3. Sew an F triangle square from step 1 to each side of a blue G square as shown. Join to the top of the unit from step 2 to form the pants unit.

4. Use the quick-corner-triangle method to sew white J squares on all the corners of a green I rectangle to make a shirt.

5. Sew the shirt unit to the pants unit and attach a white M rectangle to the bottom edge to make a body section.

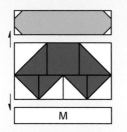

6. Sew an L rectangle unit made in step 5 of "Piecing the Paper Doll Blocks" to each side of the body section.

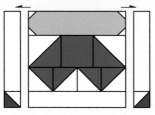

7. Attach a head section to the top edge of the shirt unit to complete the boy Paper Doll block.

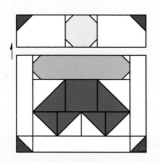

8. Repeat steps 1–7 to make two boy Paper Doll blocks with green shirts and blue pants, one with a blue shirt and blue pants, one with a purple shirt and blue pants, one with a red shirt and blue pants, and one with a blue shirt and green pants.

Piecing the Girl Paper Dolls

1. Sew a white O triangle to a bright pink O triangle to make a rectangle. Make one of each mirror image. Trim the pieced rectangles to 1½" x 2".

2. Repeat with white and bright pink S triangles, making one of each mirror image. Trim the pieced rectangles to 1½" by 2½".

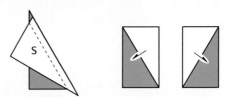

3. Sew a white R rectangle to each pieced rectangle from step 1, matching the white edges. Make one of each mirror image.

4. Place white J squares on the two corners at one end of a bright pink P rectangle as shown. Use the quick-corner-triangle method to draw, sew, press, and trim. Make two.

5. Sew a unit from step 4 to the top edge of a unit from step 3 as shown. Make one of each mirror image.

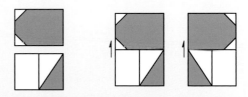

6. Sew the units from step 5 to opposite sides of a bright pink K rectangle as shown.

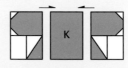

7. Sew a unit from step 2 to each end of a bright pink Q rectangle as shown. Then sew a white N rectangle to the bottom edge.

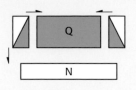

8. Sew the unit made in step 7 to the unit made in step 6 as shown to make one dress unit.

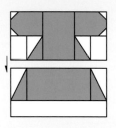

9. Sew an L rectangle unit made in step 5 of "Piecing the Paper Doll Blocks" on page 29 to each side of the dress unit made in step 8. Attach a head section to the top edge to complete the girl Paper Doll block.

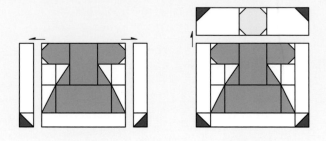

10. Repeat steps 1–9 to make two girl Paper Doll blocks with bright pink dresses, two with yellow dresses, one with a blue dress, and one with a green dress.

CUTTING FOR BORDERS AND BINDING				
Fabric	Piece	Number of Strips	Strip Width	Cut
White	B	1	1⅞"	20 squares, 1⅞" x 1⅞"
	E	1	5¼"	2 squares, 5¼" x 5¼"
	F	2	2⅞"	24 squares, 2⅞" x 2⅞"
Royal Blue	A	1	3¼"	4 squares, 3¼" x 3¼"
	B	1	1⅞"	20 squares, 1⅞" x 1⅞"
	C	1	1½"	24 squares, 1½" x 1½"
	Outer border	6	2¼"	
	Binding	6	2¼"	
Yellow	C	2	1½"	40 squares, 1½" x 1½"
Hot Pink	A	1	3¼"	4 squares, 3¼" x 3¼"
	E	1	5¼"	3 squares, 5¼" x 5¼"
	F	1	2⅞"	12 squares, 2⅞" x 2⅞"
	Inner border	5	1½"	

Piecing the Borders

1. Use the half-square-triangle technique to make triangle squares from the white and royal blue B squares. Sew them into four-patch units with the yellow C squares (see steps 1 and 2 on page 28). Make 20.

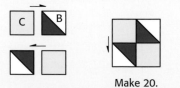

Make 20.

2. Follow steps 4 and 5 of "Piecing the Free Trade Blocks" on page 28. Use two white E squares, four hot pink A squares, and four royal blue A squares to make eight flying-geese units.

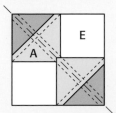

Make 8.

3. Sew four-patch units to opposite ends of the flying-geese units as shown to make section 1. Make eight. Reserve the four extra four-patch units for border corners.

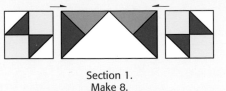

Section 1.
Make 8.

4. Using the half-square-triangle technique, place a white F square on a hot pink F square. Stitch, cut, and press. Sew 12 to make 24 triangle squares. Place a royal blue C square on the pink corner of each triangle square; stitch, press, and trim to make a quick corner triangle. Make 24.

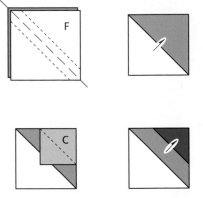

Make 24.

5. Using the flying-geese method, place white F squares on the corners of hot pink E squares. Sew three to make 12 flying-geese units.

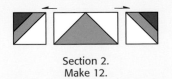

Make 12.

6. Sew pieced squares made in step 4 to opposite ends of the flying-geese units to make section 2. Make 12.

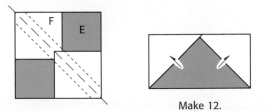

Section 2.
Make 12.

7. Sew three section 2 units and two section 1 units together as shown to make one pieced border. Repeat

to make four total. Sew four-patch corner units to both ends of two of these pieced borders.

Make 2.

Make 2.

Assembling the Quilt Top

1. Lay out the blocks in five rows of five blocks each, alternating them as shown in the quilt diagram. Join the rows.

2. Sew pieced borders without corner units to opposite sides of the quilt. Sew the pieced borders with corner units to the top and bottom edges of the quilt.

3. Sew the hot pink inner-border strips together and cut four strips, 1½" x 50". Sew the royal blue border strips together and cut four strips, 2¼" x 54". Matching midpoints, pin and sew a hot pink strip to each royal blue strip. Referring to "Mitered Corners" on page 14, sew the borders to the quilt top and miter the corners.

Finishing the Quilt

Referring to "Finishing the Quilt" on page 15, prepare the backing fabric and then layer the backing, batting, and quilt top. After basting the layers together, hand or machine quilt as desired. Bind your quilt using the 2¼"-wide royal blue strips.

Star of the Dog Show

Designed by Claudia Olson and made by Sande Tennant. Machine quilted by Sandy Ashbrook.
Finished quilt: 75" x 75" » Finished blocks: 12"

Cool and inviting sherbet colors and dogs standing at attention on their pedestals make this a quilt anyone would love to wrap up in. The prominent diagonal lines of the Jersey Star block complement the Dog Show blocks and give a continuous, pleasing flow to the quilt design.

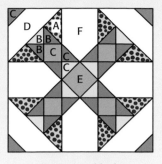

Jersey Star block

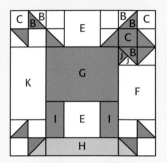

Dog Show block

Materials

Yardage is based on 42"-wide fabric.

- 3½ yards of white print for blocks and pieced border
- 2½ yards of teal print for blocks, border, and binding*
- 1¼ yards of pink print for blocks and border*
- ¾ yard of blue print for blocks and pieced border
- ¾ yard of yellow print for blocks
- ⅝ yard of hot pink print for Jersey Star blocks and pieced border
- ⅜ yard of lavender print for Dog Show blocks
- ⅜ yard of turquoise print for Dog Show blocks
- ⅜ yard of green print for Dog Show blocks
- 4½ yards of fabric for backing
- 81" x 81" piece of batting

If you prefer to cut lengthwise borders, you'll need 2⅝ yards of teal print and 2⅛ yards of pink print.

CUTTING FOR 13 JERSEY STAR BLOCKS

Fabric	Piece	Number of Strips	Strip Width	First Cut	Second Cut
Teal	B	4	2⅜"	52 squares, 2⅜" x 2⅜"	Cut all squares ◻
	C	5 and remainder of B strip	2"	104 squares, 2" x 2"	
Yellow	B	2	2⅜"	26 squares, 2⅜" x 2⅜"	Cut all squares ◻
	C	3	2"	52 squares, 2" x 2"	
Hot Pink	A	3	4¼"	26 squares, 4¼" x 4¼"	Cut all squares ⊠
Pink	C	3	2"	52 squares, 2" x 2"	
	E	2	3½"	13 squares, 3½" x 3½"	
Blue	C	3	2"	52 squares, 2" x 2"	
White	D	4	5⅜"	26 squares, 5⅜" x 5⅜"	Cut all squares ◻
	F	7	3½"	52 rectangles, 3½" x 5"	

Piecing the Jersey Star Blocks

1. Sew a teal B triangle to a yellow B triangle as shown. Sew a hot pink A triangle to the teal B triangle. Make 52.

Make 52.

2. Sew a teal B triangle to a hot pink A triangle as shown. Sew a pink C square to the end of the teal triangle. Make 52.

Make 52.

3. Sew the unit made in step 1 to the unit made in step 2 to make a large pieced triangle. Make 52.

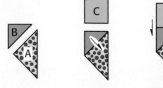

Make 52.

4. Referring to "Quick Corner Triangles" on page 11, place a blue C square on the corner of a white D triangle. Stitch, press, and trim. Make 52.

Make 52.

5. Sew the large pieced triangle made in step 3 to the triangle made in step 4. Make 52.

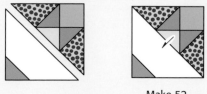

Make 52.

6. Using the quick-corner-triangle method, sew two teal C squares on one end of a white F rectangle. Make 52. Then sew yellow C squares on all the corners of a pink E square. Make 13.

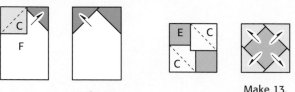

Make 52.

Make 13.

7. Lay out the pieced units as shown. Sew the units together in rows. Join the rows to complete a Jersey Star block. Make a total of 13 blocks.

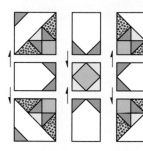
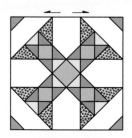

Make 13.

CUTTING FOR 12 DOG SHOW BLOCKS

Fabric	Number of Strips	Strip Width	Piece	First Cut	Second Cut
White	4	2⅜"	B	55 squares, 2⅜" x 2⅜"	
	5 and remainder of B strip	2"	C	108 squares, 2" x 2"	
	6	3½"	E	24 squares, 3½" x 3½"	
			F	12 rectangles, 3½" x 5"	
			K	12 rectangles, 3½" x 6½"	
	1	2¾"	J	6 squares, 2¾" x 2¾"	
Blue	1	2⅜"	B	12 squares, 2⅜" x 2⅜"	Cut 1 square ◻
			C	2 squares, 2" x 2"	
	1	6½"	G	2 rectangles, 5" x 6½"	
			H	6 rectangles, 2" x 6½"	
			I	4 rectangles, 2" x 3½"	
			J	1 square, 2¾" x 2¾"	
Teal	3	2⅜"	B	36 squares, 2⅜" x 2⅜"	
Green	1	2⅜"	B	10 squares, 2⅜" x 2⅜"	Cut 1 square ◻
			C	1 square, 2" x 2"	
	1	6½"	G	1 rectangle, 5" x 6½"	
			H	6 rectangles, 2" x 6½"	
			I	2 rectangles, 2" x 3½"	
			J	1 square, 2¾" x 2¾"	
Pink	1	2⅜"	B	10 squares, 2⅜" x 2⅜"	Cut 2 squares ◻
			C	3 squares, 2" x 2"	
			I	6 rectangles, 2" x 3½"	
	1	6½"	G	3 rectangles, 5" x 6½"	
			J	1 square, 2¾" x 2¾"	
Turquoise, Lavender, and Yellow	1 strip of each color	2⅜"	B	6 squares, 2⅜" x 2⅜", of each color	Cut 1 square of each color ◻
			C	2 squares, 2" x 2", of each color	
			I	4 rectangles, 2" x 3½", of each color	
	1 strip of each color	6½"	G	2 rectangles, 5" x 6½", of each color	
			J	1 square, 2¾" x 2¾", of each color	

Piecing the Dog Show Blocks

You'll make a total of 12 dog blocks: three pink, two blue, two turquoise, two lavender, two yellow, and one green. Six of the blocks have a green pedestal along the bottom, and six have blue.

1. Referring to "Quarter-Square Triangles" on page 10, position a white J square on a blue J square. Stitch on the right of the drawn lines, cut, and press. Repeat to sew one unit using each dog fabric. You'll use one triangle pair for each dog block. Sew the triangle pair to a blue B triangle (or a matching color). Repeat with each dog fabric.

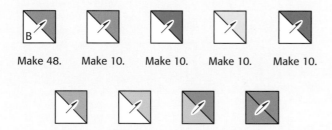

2. Referring to "Half-Square Triangles" on page 10, position a white B square on a teal B square. Stitch, cut, and press. Sew 24 to create 48 triangle squares. Repeat with B squares in the following combinations: five white/blue, five white/turquoise, five white/yellow, five white/lavender, eight white/pink, and three white/green. You need five triangle squares for each block; you'll have one extra of the white/pink and white/green combinations. Repeat again with six green B squares on six teal B squares and six blue B squares on six teal B squares to make 12 triangle squares of each combination.

Make 48.   Make 10.   Make 10.   Make 10.   Make 10.

Make 16.   Make 6.   Make 12.   Make 12.

3. Sew the teal/white triangle squares to white C squares as shown. Make 24 of each. Sew 24 of these units together as shown to make a four-patch unit. Make 12. Set the remaining 24 aside to use in step 8.

Make 24 of each.

Make 12.

4. Join three blue/white triangle squares to three white C squares. Make two with the blue triangle on the left and one with the blue triangle on the right.

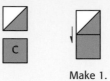

Make 2.   Make 1.

5. Sew a blue/white triangle square to a blue C square. Make one.

Make 1.

6. Sew one of each unit together as shown to make the top of the dog's ear and nose. Repeat steps 4–6 to make one unit for each Dog Show block.

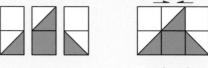

Make 1 for each block.

7. Sew the green/teal triangle squares and the blue/teal triangle squares together with white C squares as shown. Make 12 of each.

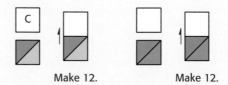

Make 12.   Make 12.

8. Sew the units made in step 7 to the teal/white two-patch units made in step 3. Make 12 of each four-patch unit. The teal/green four-patch units will be used for the blocks with green pedestals and the teal/blue four-patch units will be used for the blocks with blue pedestals.

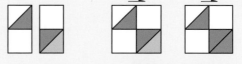

Make 12 of each.

9. Sew a blue unit made in step 1 to a blue/white triangle square as shown. Make one for each block. Repeat for each dog fabric.

10. Join the remaining unit made in step 4 (blue triangle on the left) to a four-patch unit made in step 3 as shown. Make one for each dog fabric.

11. Sew blue I rectangles on opposite sides of a white E square. Sew a blue G rectangle to the top of this unit and a green H rectangle on the bottom. Make one for each block, using either a blue or green H rectangle.

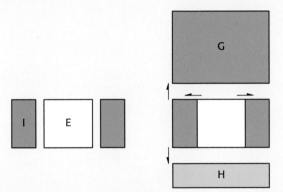

12. Sew a teal/green four-patch unit made in step 8 to the bottom of a white K rectangle.

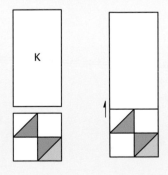

13. Sew a white F rectangle between a teal/green four-patch unit and a unit from step 9 as shown. Repeat for each block, being careful to match the pedestal color to the green or blue triangle.

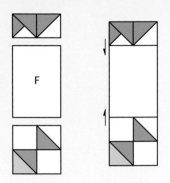

14. Sew units from steps 12 and 13 to opposite sides of a unit made in step 11 to make a dog body. Repeat for each block.

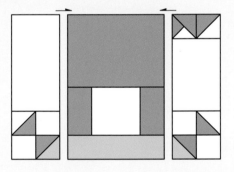

15. Sew the units made in steps 6 and 10 to opposite sides of a white E square as shown.

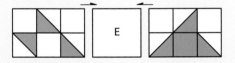

16. Sew the dog body to the bottom of the unit made in step 15 to complete a Dog Show block. Make two blue, two yellow, two turquoise, two lavender, three pink, and one green for a total of 12 Dog Show blocks.

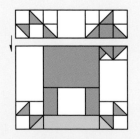
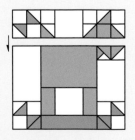

CUTTING FOR BORDERS AND BINDING

Fabric	Piece	Number of Strips	Strip Width	First Cut	Second Cut
White	B	2	2⅜"	32 squares, 2⅜" x 2⅜"	
	C	3	2"	48 squares, 2" x 2"	
	H	2	2"	12 rectangles, 2" x 6½"	
	L	1	3⅞"	8 squares, 3⅞" x 3⅞"	Cut all squares ◻
Teal	B	2	2⅜"	24 squares, 2⅜" x 2⅜"	
	C	1 and remainder of B strip	2"	24 squares, 2" x 2"	
	M	1	2⅝"	8 squares, 2⅝" x 2⅝"	
	Border	8	3¼"		
	Binding	8	2¼"		
Blue	B	1	2⅜"	10 squares, 2⅜" x 2⅜"	
	H	2	2"	12 rectangles, 2" x 6½"	
Pink	B	1	2⅜"	2 squares, 2⅜" x 2⅜"	
	C	2 and remainder of B strip	2"	60 squares, 2" x 2"	
	Border	8	2"		
Hot Pink	A	1	4¼"	4 squares, 4¼" x 4¼"	Cut all squares ⊠

Piecing the Borders

1. Using the half-square-triangle technique, position 24 white B squares on 24 teal B squares. Draw, sew, cut, and press to make 48 triangle squares. Repeat with eight white and eight blue B squares and with two pink and two blue B squares.

Make 48.   Make 16.   Make 4.

2. Join the teal/white triangle squares to white C squares and pink C squares as shown. Make 24 four-patch units. Join blue/white triangle squares to white C squares and pink C squares to make 16 four-patch units. Join blue/pink triangle squares to white C squares and pink C squares to make four four-patch units for the corners.

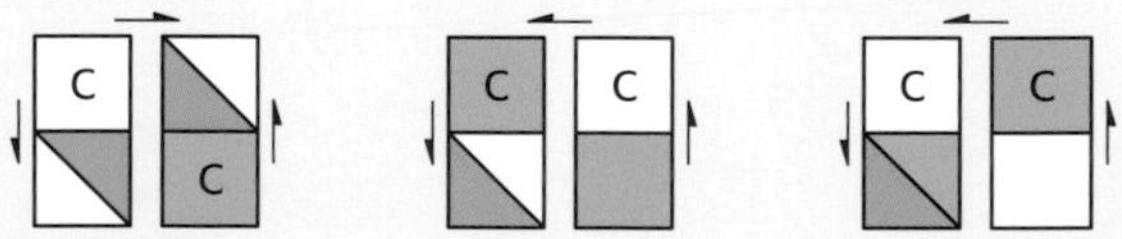

Make 24.   Make 16.   Make 4.

3. Use the quick-corner-triangle technique to sew a teal C square to each end of a blue H rectangle. Then sew a white H rectangle to the unit as shown. Make 12.

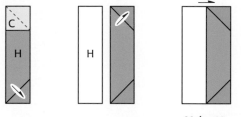

Make 12.

4. Sew a teal/white four-patch unit made in step 2 to each end of the unit made in step 3 to make section 1. Make 12.

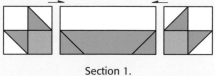

Section 1.
Make 12.

5. Sew hot pink A triangles to adjacent sides of a teal M square. Add white L triangles to the sides. Repeat to make eight.

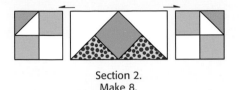

Make 8.

6. Sew the blue/white/pink four-patch units made in step 2 to opposite ends of the unit made in step 5 to complete section 2. Make 8.

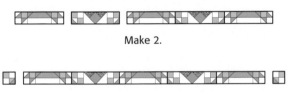

Section 2.
Make 8.

7. Sew three section 1 units and two section 2 units together, alternating them as shown to make one pieced border. Repeat to make four borders. Sew the corner squares made in step 2 to each end of two of the pieced borders.

Make 2.

Make 2.

Assembling the Quilt Top

1. Arrange the blocks in five rows of five blocks each, alternating them as shown in the quilt diagram.

2. Sew the pieced borders without corner squares to opposite sides of the quilt. Sew the pieced borders with corner squares to the top and bottom edges of the quilt.

3. Sew the pink border strips together and cut four strips, 2" x 72". Sew the teal border strips together and cut four strips, 3¼" x 79".

4. Referring to "Mitered Corners" on page 14, match the centers of the 2" pink borders and the 3¼" teal borders, pin, and sew them together. Sew them to the quilt top and miter the corners.

Finishing the Quilt

Referring to "Finishing the Quilt" on page 15, prepare the backing fabric and then layer the backing, batting, and quilt top. After basting the layers together, hand or machine quilt as desired. Bind your quilt using the 2¼"-wide teal strips.

Alaskan Ducks

Designed by Claudia Olson and made by Linda Krueger. Machine quilted by Linda Krueger.
Finished quilt: 72½" x 72½" » Finished blocks: 12"

A traditional Duck block has been altered to make the duck appear to be the solitary figure often seen floating on southeast Alaskan waters. The Alaska Territory block provides coastal mountains in the background. The natural blues and greens give this quilt an outdoorsy feeling, perfect for nature lovers.

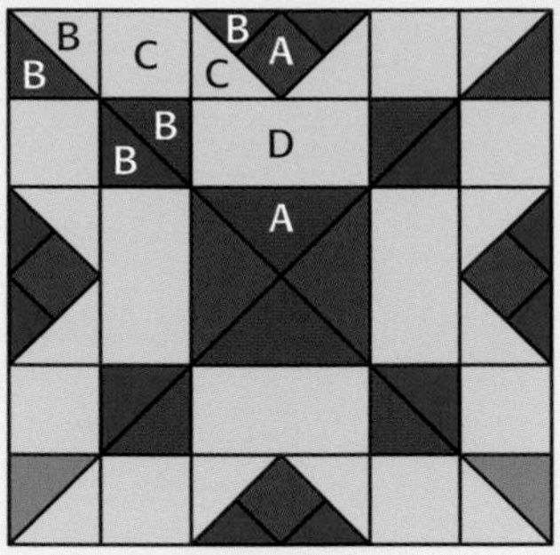

Alaska Territory block

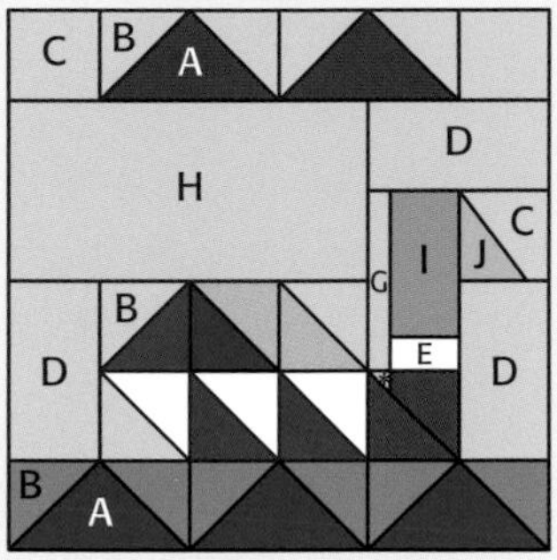

Duck block
* *Indicates piece F*

Materials

Yardage is based on 42"-wide fabric.

- 3⅞ yards of sky blue fabric for blocks and borders
- 2½ yards of dark blue print for blocks, border, and binding
- 1½ yards of brown print for blocks and border
- 1 yard of dark green print for blocks and borders
- ⅝ yard of teal print for blocks and border
- ¼ yard of royal blue print for Duck blocks
- ¼ yard of black print for Duck blocks
- ¼ yard of beige print for Duck blocks
- ¼ yard of white fabric for Duck blocks
- ¼ yard of kelly green print for Duck blocks
- ¼ yard of gold print for Duck blocks
- 4½ yards of fabric for backing
- 79" x 79" piece of batting

CUTTING FOR 13 ALASKA TERRITORY BLOCKS

Fabric	Piece	Number of Strips	Strip Width	Cut
Sky Blue	B	2	2⅞"	26 squares, 2⅞" x 2⅞"
	C	13	2½"	208 squares, 2½" x 2½"
	D	4	4½"	52 rectangles, 2½" x 4½"
Brown	A	3	5¼"	20 squares, 5¼" x 5¼"
	B	1	2⅞"	13 squares, 2⅞" x 2⅞"
Teal	B	1	2⅞"	13 squares, 2⅞" x 2⅞"
Dark Blue	B	6	2⅞"	78 squares, 2⅞" x 2⅞"
Dark Green	A	1	5¼"	7 squares, 5¼" x 5¼"
	B	2	2⅞"	26 squares, 2⅞" x 2⅞"

Piecing the Alaska Territory Blocks

1. Referring to "Half-Square Triangles" on page 10, layer a sky blue B square on a brown B square. Stitch, cut, and press. Sew 13 to create 26 triangle squares. Repeat with 13 sky blue and teal B squares to make 26 triangle squares, and then repeat with 26 dark blue and dark green B squares to make 52 triangle squares.

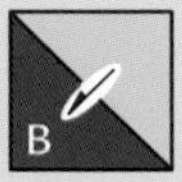

Make 26.

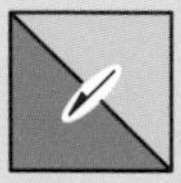

Make 26.

Make 52.

2. Referring to "Quarter-Square Triangles" on page 10, place a dark green A square on a brown A square. Draw, stitch to the left of the drawn line, cut, and press. Sew seven to produce 28 triangle pairs; two will be extra. Sew the triangle pairs together as shown to make 13 center squares.

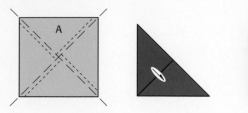

Make 13.

3. Referring to "Flying-Geese Units" on page 12, sew dark blue B squares on the corners of a brown A square. Stitch, cut, and press. Sew 13 to create 52 flying-geese units.

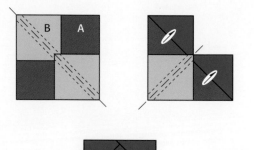

Make 52.

4. Referring to "Quick Corner Triangles" on page 11, sew a sky blue C square on the end of the flying-geese unit just made. Sew a sky blue C square on the other end of the unit; then sew a sky blue D rectangle to the bottom of the unit. Make 52.

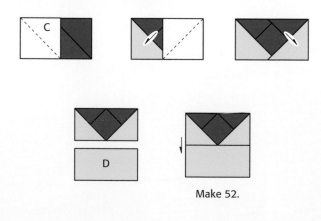

Make 52.

5. Sew the triangle squares made in step 1 to sky blue C squares; then sew the pairs together, following the placement below. Note that they are mirror images. Make 13 of each.

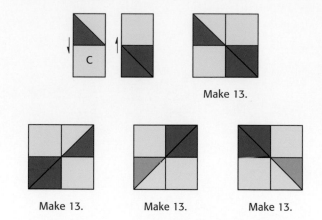

Make 13.

Make 13.   Make 13.   Make 13.

6. Lay out the units made in steps 2, 4, and 5 in rows as shown. Sew the units into rows, and then join the rows to complete the Alaska Territory blocks. Make 13.

Make 13.

Piecing the Duck Blocks

1. Referring to "Half-Square Triangles" on page 10, layer a white B square on a black B square. Stitch, cut, and press. Repeat with sky blue and black B squares, royal blue and beige B squares, sky blue and beige B squares, sky blue and white B squares, and black and beige B squares. Sew six of each combination to create 12 triangle squares each.

Make 12 of each.

CUTTING FOR 12 DUCK BLOCKS

Fabric	Piece	Number of Strips	Strip Width	First Cut	Second Cut
White	B	1	2⅞"	12 squares, 2⅞" x 2⅞"	
	E	1	2"	12 rectangles, 1¼" x 2"	
Black	B	2	2⅞"	18 squares, 2⅞" x 2⅞"	
Sky Blue	B	4	2⅞"	42 squares, 2⅞" x 2⅞"	
	C	2 and remainder of B strip	2½"	36 squares, 2½" x 2½"	
	D	3	4½"	36 rectangles, 2½" x 4½"	
	F	1	1½"	12 squares, 1½" x 1½"	
	G	2	1"	12 rectangles, 1" x 4½"	
	H	3	4½"	12 rectangles, 4½" x 8½"	
Royal Blue	B	1	2⅞"	6 squares, 2⅞" x 2⅞"	
Beige	B	2	2⅞"	18 squares, 2⅞" x 2⅞"	
Brown	B	1	2⅞"	12 squares, 2⅞" x 2⅞"	Cut all squares ◺
Kelly Green	I	1	3¾"	12 rectangles, 2" x 3¾"	
Gold	J	1	3½"	12 rectangles, 2" x 3½"	
Dark Blue	A	2	5½"	9 squares, 5½" x 5½"	
Dark Green	A	1	5¼"	6 squares, 5¼" x 5¼"	
Teal	B	3	2⅞"	36 squares, 2⅞" x 2⅞"	

2. Sew the triangle squares made in step 1 together in pairs as shown. Sew the pairs together and attach a sky blue D rectangle to the left end to make a body unit. Make 12.

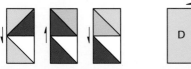

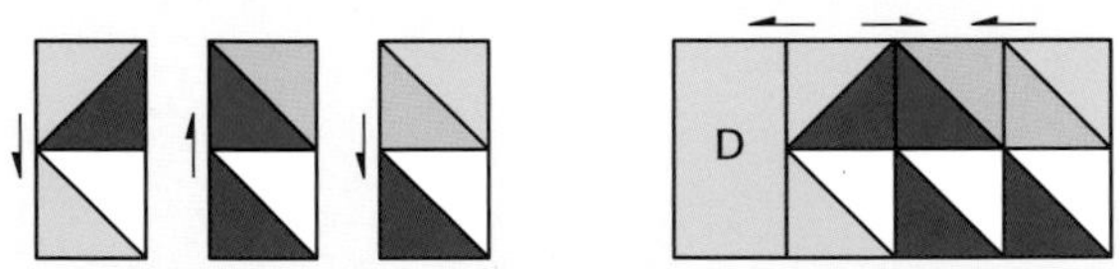

Make 12.

3. Referring to "Paper Foundation Piecing" on page 12, use the lower neck unit foundation pattern on page 49 to make a paper foundation. Place a precut brown B triangle on the foundation. Lay a sky blue F square over the drawn line and sew on the line. Fold over the sky blue square and press. Trim the sky blue square along the edges of the brown triangle, being careful to include seam allowances. Gently remove the paper foundation. Then sew another brown B triangle to the paper-pieced unit as shown. Make 12.

Make 12.

4. Sew a white E rectangle to the bottom end of a kelly green I rectangle. Then sew a sky blue G rectangle to the left side of the unit. Make 12.

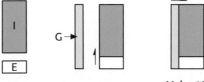

Make 12.

5. Sew the unit from step 3 to the lower end of the unit from step 4 to make a neck unit. Make 12.

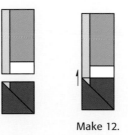

Make 12.

6. Use the beak unit foundation pattern on page 49 to make a paper foundation. Place a sky blue C square on the paper foundation. Lay a gold J rectangle over the drawn line and sew on the line. Fold over the gold rectangle and press. Trim the rectangle, being careful to include seam allowances. Gently remove the paper pattern. Sew a sky blue D rectangle below the beak unit as shown. Make 12.

Make 12.

7. Sew the neck unit from step 5 to the left edge of the beak unit from step 6. Sew a sky blue D rectangle to the top of this new unit. Make 12.

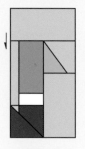
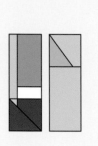
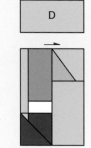

Make 12.

8. Sew a sky blue H rectangle to the body unit made in step 2. Attach the unit made in step 7 to complete a duck unit. Make 12.

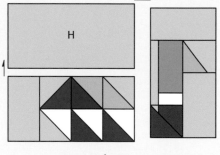

Make 12.

9. Referring to "Flying-Geese Units" on page 12, place sky blue B squares on the corners of a dark green A square. Draw, stitch, cut, and press. Sew six to create

24 sky blue/dark green flying-geese units. Repeat by sewing teal B squares on the corners of dark blue A squares. Sew nine to produce 36 teal/dark blue flying-geese units.

Make 24.

Make 36.

10. Sew two sky blue/dark green flying-geese units together. Sew a sky blue C square to each end. Make 12.

Make 12.

11. Sew three teal/dark blue flying-geese units together. Make 12.

Make 12.

12. Sew units made in steps 10 and 11 to the top and bottom edges of the duck unit as shown to complete a Duck block. Make 12.

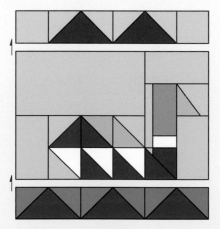

Make 12.

CUTTING FOR BORDERS AND BINDING

Fabric	Piece	Number of Strips	Strip Width	Cut
Dark Blue	A	1	5¼"	6 squares, 5¼" x 5¼"
	B	2	2⅞"	16 squares, 2⅞" x 2⅞"
	D	1 and remainder of B strip	4½"	16 rectangles, 2½" x 4½"
	K	2	2½"	4 rectangles, 2½" x 12½"
	M	4	2½"	8 rectangles, 2½" x 20"
	Binding	8	2¼"	
Brown	A	1	5¼"	2 squares, 5¼" x 5¼"
	B	1	2⅞"	8 squares, 2⅞" x 2⅞"
	C	1	2½"	16 squares, 2½" x 2½"
	K	2	2½"	4 rectangles, 2½" x 12½"
	L	4	2½"	8 rectangles, 2½" x 18"
Sky Blue	A	1	5¼"	3 squares, 5¼" x 5¼"
	B	2 and remainder of A strip	2⅞"	28 squares, 2⅞" x 2⅞"
	C	3	2½"	36 squares, 2½" x 2½"
	D	1	2½"	8 rectangles, 2½" x 4½"
Teal	B	1	2⅞"	4 squares, 2⅞" x 2⅞"
Dark Green	A	1	5¼"	2 squares, 5¼" x 5¼"
	B	2 and remainder of A strip	2⅞"	28 squares, 2⅞" x 2⅞"

Piecing the Borders

There are three pieced borders on this quilt. Border 1 is made of sections 1 and 2, border 2 is made of section 3, and border 3 is made of section 4.

Piecing Section 1

1. Referring to steps 3 and 4 of "Piecing the Alaska Territory Blocks" on page 44, make eight pieced rectangles as shown using the dark blue B squares, the brown A squares, and the sky blue C squares.

Make 8.

2. Sew a sky blue C square to both ends of each unit just made.

C

3. Using the half-square-triangle technique, place a sky blue B square on a teal B square. Stitch, cut, and press. Repeat with sky blue B squares on dark green

B squares. Sew four of each to make eight triangle squares of each combination.

Make 8.    Make 8.

4. Sew the triangle squares made in step 3 to each end of the units made in step 2 as shown. Make two of each variation for a total of eight units.

Left side border section.   Right side border section.
Make 2.   Make 2.

Top border section.   Bottom border section.
Make 2.   Make 2.

Piecing Section 2

1. Use the flying-geese technique. Position dark green B squares on three sky blue A squares. Make 12 flying-geese units.

Make 12.

2. Repeat with dark green B squares on three dark blue A squares. After you have cut and pressed the first time, sew a sky blue B square to the remaining corner of each dark blue A square. Make 12 of each mirror image.

Make 12.   Make 12.

3. Sew one of each flying-geese unit made in step 2 to each end of the flying-geese units made in step 1 as shown. Make 12.

Make 12.

Piecing Section 3

1. Using the half-square-triangle technique, position a sky blue B square on a brown B square. Stitch, cut, and press eight pairs of squares to create 16 triangle squares.

Make 16.

2. Sew a triangle square made in step 1 to each end of a sky blue D rectangle. Then sew a brown C square to each end. Make eight.

Make 8.

Piecing Section 4

1. Using the flying-geese technique, place dark blue B squares on a dark green A square. Sew two to make eight flying-geese units.

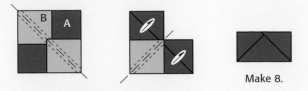

Make 8.

2. Sew a dark blue D rectangle to each end of the flying-geese units. Make eight.

Make 8.

Making Border 1

1. To make the top border, sew three section 2 units to two section 1 units (with two dark green triangle squares), alternating them as shown. Label the border unit *top*.

Border 1 top

2. To make the bottom border, sew three section 2 units to two section 1 units (with two teal triangle squares), alternating them as shown. Label the border unit *bottom*.

Border 1 bottom

3. To make the left border, sew three section 2 units to two section 1 units (with teal triangle squares on the left and dark green triangle squares on the right), alternating them as shown. Label the border unit *left*. Sew a sky blue C square to each end of the border.

Border 1 left

4. To make the right border, sew three section 2 units to two section 1 units (with dark green triangle squares on the left and teal triangle squares on the right), alternating them as shown. Label the border unit *right*. Sew a sky blue C square to each end of the border.

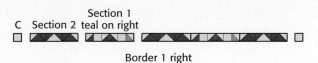

Border 1 right

Making Border 2

Sew a section 3 unit to each end of a brown K rectangle; then sew a brown L rectangle to each end. Make four.

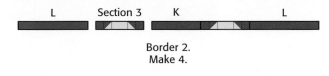

Border 2.
Make 4.

Making Border 3

Sew a section 4 unit to each end of a dark blue K rectangle; then sew a dark blue M rectangle to each end. Make four.

M   Section 4   K   M
Border 3.
Make 4.

Assembling the Quilt Top

1. Arrange the blocks in five rows of five blocks each, alternating them as shown in the quilt diagram. Sew the five rows together.

2. Sew the top and bottom border 1 units to the quilt. Sew the left and right border 1 units (with corner squares) to the sides of the quilt, being careful to align the teal triangle squares with the water for the duck.

3. Sew two border 2 units to the top and bottom edges of the quilt, starting and stopping ¼" away from the end. Don't trim the ends of the brown L rectangles. Sew the remaining two border 2 units to the sides of the quilt in the same manner.

4. Sew two border 3 units to the top and bottom edges of the quilt. Don't trim the ends of the dark blue M rectangles. Sew the remaining two border 3 units to the sides of the quilt in the same manner.

5. Referring to "Mitered Corners" on page 14, miter the corners of the borders.

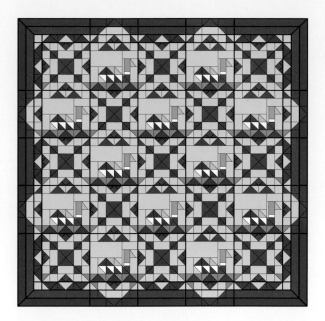

Finishing the Quilt

Referring to "Finishing the Quilt" on page 15, prepare the backing fabric and then layer the backing, batting, and quilt top. After basting the layers together, hand or machine quilt as desired. Bind your quilt using the 2¼"-wide dark blue strips.

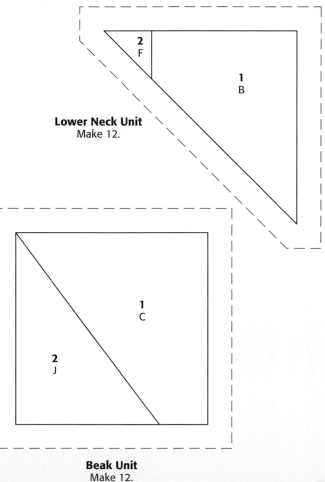

Lower Neck Unit
Make 12.

Beak Unit
Make 12.

Albany Giraffes

Designed and made by Claudia Olson. Machine quilted by Jill Therriault.
Finished quilt: 77" x 77" » Finished blocks: 12"

This quilt pairs Albany variation blocks with Giraffe Trio blocks, an original design that my son helped to create. The large-scale character print featured in the Albany blocks contains giraffes, but any African print would work just as well. The bright prints and animal motifs will make any room sizzle with tropical flavor.

Materials

Yardage is based on 42"-wide fabric.

- 2½ yards of animal print for outer border*
- 2⅜ yards of white print for blocks and pieced border
- 1⅝ yards of violet print for Albany blocks and inner border**
- 1⅜ yards of yellow print for blocks and pieced border
- 1⅛ yards of multicolored small pebble print for baby giraffes and binding
- 1 yard of giraffe print for Albany blocks†
- ⅞ yard of blue-and-pink large pebble print for large giraffes‡
- ¾ yard of red print for Albany blocks and pieced border
- ¾ yard of orange print for Albany blocks and pieced border
- ¾ yard of yellow-and-orange medium pebble print for medium giraffes
- ⅝ yard of green print for Albany blocks and pieced border
- 4¾ yards of fabric for backing
- 83" x 83" piece of batting
- Embroidery floss in black and in colors to match chosen fabrics

This is for cutting all strips lengthwise. If your print is directional and you need to cut the top and bottom strips crosswise, purchase 2¾ yards.

**If you prefer to cut lengthwise borders, you'll need 2 yards.*

†*Extra fabric is included for fussy cutting.*

‡*The multicolored fabric used in this quilt allowed for cutting both blue and pink giraffes. Purchase ½ yard each of two different fabrics if you want to cut two different-colored giraffes.*

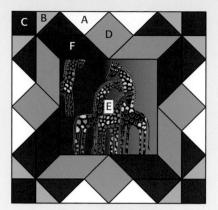

Albany Variation block

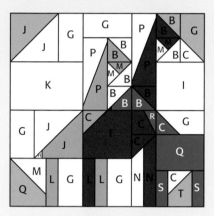

Giraffe Trio block

CUTTING FOR 13 ALBANY BLOCKS

Fabric	Piece	Number of Strips	Strip Width	First Cut	Second Cut
White	A	3	4¼"	26 squares, 4¼" x 4¼"	Cut all squares ⊠
Green	D	4	2⅝"	52 squares, 2⅝" x 2⅝"	
Yellow	B	4	2⅜"	52 squares, 2⅜" x 2⅜"	Cut all squares ◱
Violet	C	3	2"	52 squares, 2" x 2"	
	F	3	5"	52 rectangles, 2" x 5"	See next page.
Red	A	3	4¼"	26 squares, 4¼" x 4¼"	Cut all squares ⊠
Orange	F	3	5"	52 rectangles, 2" x 5"	See next page.
Giraffe Print	E	3*	6½"	13 squares, 6½" x 6½"	
Don't cut strips if you plan to fussy cut the squares.					

Second Cut with Template

For the violet and orange F pieces, use a template made from quickie template pattern 1 on page 60. Layer the rectangles right sides up and cut off 1⅝" corners as shown. Don't cut with wrong sides together or you'll get wrong-facing parallelograms.

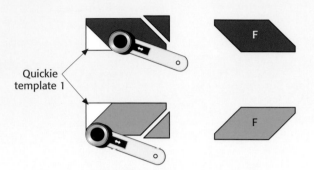

Quickie template 1

Piecing the Albany Blocks

1. Sew white A triangles to two sides of a green D square as shown. Sew yellow B triangles to two sides of a violet C square. Make 52 of each.

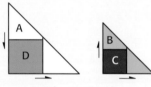

Make 52 of each.

2. Sew red A triangles to the top edge of a violet F parallelogram and the top edge of an orange F parallelogram. Sew the two different units to opposite sides of a green/white unit made in step 1. Repeat to make 52.

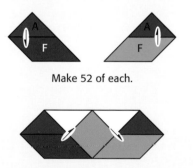

Make 52 of each.

Make 52.

3. Sew two units made in step 2 to the top and bottom edges of a giraffe print E square, starting and stopping ¼" from the ends to allow for set-in seams. Backstitch to secure the seam. Sew two units to the sides of the E square in the same manner. Then sew the diagonal seam from the corner to the end of the red triangles. Make 13 units.

Start and stop ¼" from ends.

Make 13.

4. Sew the yellow/violet units from step 1 to the corners of the unit just made to complete the Albany Variation block. Make 13.

Make 13.

CUTTING FOR 12 GIRAFFE TRIO BLOCKS

Fabric	Piece	Number of Strips	Strip Width	First Cut	Second Cut
White	B	2	2⅜"	30 squares, 2⅜" x 2⅜"	Cut 18 squares ◹
	C	2	2"	24 squares, 2" x 2"	
	G	4	3½"	72 rectangles, 2" x 3½"	
	H	1	1¼"	12 squares, 1¼" x 1¼"	
	I	1 and remainder of G strip	3½"	12 squares, 3½" x 3½"	
	J	2	3⅞"	12 squares, 3⅞" x 3⅞"	Cut 6 squares ◹
	K	2	3½"	12 rectangles, 3½" x 5"	
	M	2	2¾"	18 squares, 2¾" x 2¾"	
	N	1 and remainder of H strip	1¼"	12 rectangles, 1¼" x 5"	
	P	2	2¼"	12 rectangles, 2¼" x 6½"	Cut all rectangles ◹ *
Yellow	B	1	2⅜"	6 squares, 2⅜" x 2⅜"	
	G	1	3½"	12 rectangles, 2" x 3½"	
	J	1	3⅞"	6 squares, 3⅞" x 3⅞"	
	Q	1 and remainder of G strip	2¾"	12 rectangles, 2¾" x 3½"	
	T	1	2"	12 rectangles, 2" x 2¾"	
Yellow-and-Orange Medium Pebble Print	B	1	2⅜"	6 squares, 2⅜" x 2⅜"	
	C	1	2"	12 squares, 2" x 2"	
	J	1	3⅞"	6 squares, 3⅞" x 3⅞"	Cut all squares ◹ and then use template (see next page).
	L	1	3½"	24 rectangles, 1¼" x 3½"	
	M	1	2¾"	3 squares, 2¾" x 2¾"	
	P	1	2¼"	6 rectangles, 2¼" x 6½"	Cut all rectangles ◹ *
	Tails	5	⅛"	60 pieces, 2" to 3" long	
	Ears	Cut 24 ear shapes using the pattern on page 60.			
Blue-and-Pink Large Pebble Print	B	1	2⅜"	12 squares, 2⅜" x 2⅜"	
	C	2	2"	24 squares, 2" x 2"	
	I	2	3½"	12 squares, 3½" x 3½"	
	L	1	3½"	12 rectangles, 1¼" x 3½"	
	M	Remainder of L strip	2¾"	3 squares, 2¾" x 2¾"	
	N	2	1¼"	12 rectangles, 1¼" x 5"	
	O	Remainder of N strip	¾"	12 squares, ¾" x ¾"	
	P	1	2¼"	6 rectangles, 2¼" x 6½"	Cut all rectangles ◹ *
	Tails	5	⅛"	60 pieces, 2" to 3" long	
	Ears	Cut 24 ear shapes using the pattern on page 60.			

*To cut rectangles, layer them right sides up and cut diagonally from corner to corner.
Don't cut with wrong sides together or you'll get wrong-facing triangles.*

continued on page 54

CUTTING FOR 12 GIRAFFE TRIO BLOCKS

Fabric	Piece	Number of Strips	Strip Width	First Cut	Second Cut
Multicolored Small Pebble Print	B	1	2⅜"	12 squares, 2⅜" x 2⅜"	Cut 6 squares ◻ and then use template (see below).
	C	1	2"	12 squares, 2" x 2"	
	Q	2	2¾"	12 rectangles, 2¾" x 3½"	
	R	1	1½"	12 rectangles, 1½" x 2¾"	
	S	Remainder of Q strip	2¾"	24 rectangles, 1¼" x 2¾"	
	Tails	4	⅛"	60 pieces, 2" to 2½" long	
	Ears	Cut 24 ear shapes using the pattern on page 60.			

Second Cut with Templates

For the yellow-and-orange J and multicolored B triangles, you need to cut the points off the triangles. Use templates made from quickie template patterns 2 and 3 on page 60. Layer the triangles right sides up and cut the corner off as shown. Don't cut with wrong sides together or you'll get wrong-facing triangles. Use template 2 for the J triangles and template 3 for the B triangles.

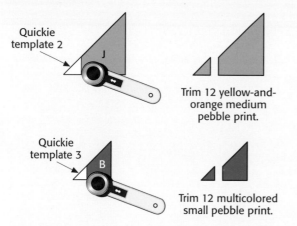

Quickie template 2

Trim 12 yellow-and-orange medium pebble print.

Quickie template 3

Trim 12 multicolored small pebble print.

Piecing the Giraffe Trio Blocks

The steps that follow are for making all 12 Giraffe Trio blocks the same.

1. Referring to "Half-Square Triangles" on page 10, place a white J square on a yellow J square. Stitch, cut, and press. Repeat with a white B square on a yellow-and-orange B square, a yellow B square on a blue-and-pink B square, and a multicolored B square on a blue-and-pink B square. Sew six of each to make 12 half-square triangles of each combination.

Make 12.　Make 12.　Make 12.　Make 12.

2. Sew same-colored ear shapes right sides together using a ⅛" seam; then turn the ears right side out. Make 36 (12 of each color). Using a seam ripper, carefully undo several stitches of the 12 multicolored/blue-and-pink triangle squares made in step 1. Insert a matching ear ½" from the top edge and resew the seam.

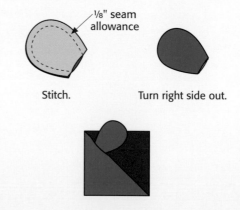

⅛" seam allowance

Stitch.　　Turn right side out.

3. Place five yellow-and-orange tail strips right sides together along the trimmed edge of a yellow-and-orange J triangle. Place a white H square along the edge, sew, and press. Place a rotary-cutting ruler along the diagonal edge of the J triangle and trim the

H square. Sew this unit to a white J triangle. Repeat with a blue-and-pink O square on a trimmed multi-colored B triangle, but don't include the tail strips. Instead, add a white B triangle. Make 12 of each.

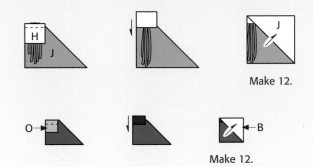

Make 12.

Make 12.

4. Sew a white G rectangle to the right side of a white/yellow J triangle square made in step 1. Then sew a white G rectangle to the left of a triangle square with a tail made in step 3 as shown. Sew a white K rectangle between the two units to make the top of row 1 (the rows are vertical). Make 12.

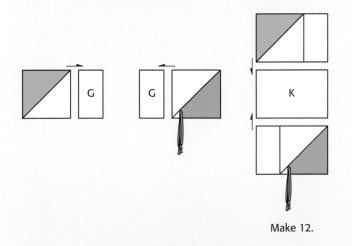

Make 12.

5. Referring to "Quarter-Square Triangles" on page 10, layer a white M square on a yellow-and-orange M square. Draw, sew to the right of the lines, cut, and press. Repeat with a white M square on a blue-and-pink M square. Sew three of each to make 12 of each

finished unit. Then sew a white B triangle to the lower edge of the triangle pairs as shown to make the giraffe chins.

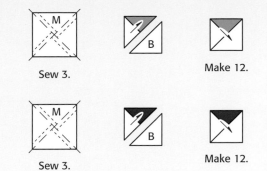

Sew 3.   Make 12.

Sew 3.   Make 12.

6. Lay out and sew together quarter-square units from step 5 and half-square units from steps 1 and 3 as shown to make the giraffe noses. Make 12 of each.

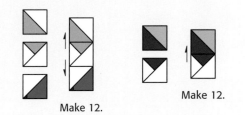

Make 12.   Make 12.

7. Sew a white P triangle to a yellow-and-orange P triangle; then sew a white P triangle to a blue-and-pink P triangle. Press and trim the rectangles to 2" x 5". Pick out a few stitches and insert a matching ear ½" from the top edge. Resew the seam. Make 12 of each.

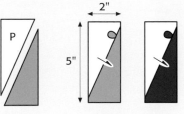

Make 12 of each.

8. Sew the yellow-and-orange pieced rectangle made in step 7 to the left side of the yellow-and-orange nose unit made in step 6 as shown. Then sew a white G rectangle to the top edge. Make 12.

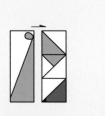

Make 12.

9. Referring to "Quick Corner Triangles" on page 11, place a white C square on the lower edge of a yellow G rectangle, sewing from upper left to lower right. Press and trim. Repeat to sew a yellow-and-orange C square on the upper-left corner of a blue-and-pink I square, a multicolored C square on the lower-left corner of a white G rectangle, a white C square on the upper-left corner of a yellow T rectangle, and a white M square on the upper-right corner of a yellow Q rectangle. Make 12 of each.

Make 12 of each.

10. Referring to "Paper Foundation Piecing" on page 12, use the foundation pattern on page 60 to make a paper foundation. Use a multicolored R rectangle and a blue-and-pink C square as shown to sew and trim a baby giraffe neck. Gently remove the paper foundation. Repeat to make 12.

Make 12.

11. To make the baby giraffe legs, sew a multicolored S rectangle on each side of a white-cornered yellow T rectangle made in step 9. Make 12.

Make 12.

12. Sew a yellow-and-orange L rectangle to the right of a white-cornered yellow Q rectangle made in step 9. Then sew a white G rectangle to the right side of the unit. Sew this unit to the bottom edge of the unit from step 4 to complete row 1. Make 12.

Row 1.
Make 12.

13. Sew a blue-and-pink N rectangle to a white N rectangle. Sew a blue-and-pink C square to the upper-left corner of the pair to make tall giraffe legs. Make 12.

Make 12.

14. Sew a blue-and-pink L rectangle to a yellow-and-orange L rectangle. Sew a white G rectangle to the right edge of the pair to make medium giraffe legs. Sew this unit to the bottom of the yellow-and-orange-cornered I square made in step 9. Make 12.

Make 12.

15. Sew a unit with the yellow-and-orange giraffe neck and head made in step 8 to the top of the unit made in step 14 to make row 2 of the block. Repeat to make 12.

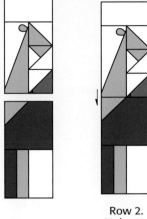

Row 2.
Make 12.

16. Sew the blue-and-pink P half-rectangle to the top of the multicolored/blue-and-pink triangle square with an ear. Sew the paper-pieced square made in step 10 to the lower edge of the unit. Last, add the tall giraffe legs to the bottom of the unit to make row 3. Repeat to make 12.

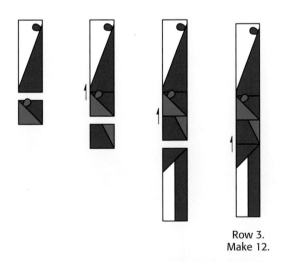

Row 3.
Make 12.

17. Sew a white-cornered yellow G rectangle made in step 9 to the right edge of a small nose unit. Repeat to make 12.

Make 12.

18. Sew the multicolored-cornered white G rectangle made in step 9 to the top edge of a multicolored Q rectangle. Then sew the baby giraffe legs to the lower edge of the unit to make a baby giraffe body. Make 12.

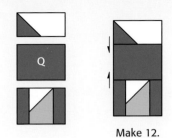

Make 12.

19. Sew a white I square between the baby giraffe body and the nose unit made in step 17 to make row 4. Make 12. Sew five multicolored tail strips to the right edge of the Q rectangles.

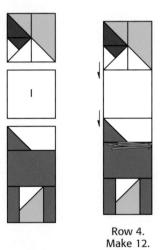

Row 4.
Make 12.

20. Lay out the rows of the block as shown and sew them together, inserting blue-and-pink tail strips in the seam for the tall giraffe. Embroider the eyes and bony knobs on the giraffe heads with black thread using a stem stitch and French knots. (See "Embellishing" on page 13.) If the baby giraffe needs more definition, outline it with a stem stitch and matching thread. Repeat to make 12 Giraffe Trio blocks.

Make 12.

CUTTING FOR BORDERS AND BINDING

Fabric	Piece	Number of Strips	Strip Width	First Cut	Second Cut
Yellow	B	2	2⅜"	20 squares, 2⅜" x 2⅜"	Cut all squares ◺
	J	2	3⅞"	12 squares, 3⅞" x 3⅞"	
Red	A	1	4¼"	4 squares, 4¼" x 4¼"	Cut all squares ⊠
	J	1 and remainder of A strip	3⅞"	12 squares, 3⅞" x 3⅞"	
White	A	2	4¼"	10 squares, 4¼" x 4¼"	Cut all squares ⊠
Green	D	2	2⅝"	20 squares, 2⅝" x 2⅝"	
Violet	C	1	2"	20 squares, 2" x 2"	
	F	1	5"	16 rectangles, 2" x 5"	See below.
	J	2	3⅞"	14 squares, 3⅞" x 3⅞"	Cut all squares ◺
	Border	8	2"	(Or cut 4 strips, 2" x 72")	
Orange	A	1	4¼"	4 squares, 4¼" x 4¼"	Cut all squares ⊠
Animal Print	Border	4 lengthwise strips	4¼" x 81"		
Multicolored Small Pebble Print	Binding	8	2¼"		

Second Cut with Template

For the violet F rectangles, use a template made from quickie template pattern 1 on page 60. Layer the rectangles wrong sides together and cut off 1⅝" corners as shown. This time, *do* cut with wrong sides together so that you'll get opposite-facing parallelograms.

Quickie template 1

Piecing the Borders

1. Referring to "Half-Square Triangles" on page 10, place a yellow J square on a red J square. Stitch, cut, and press. Sew 12 to make 24.

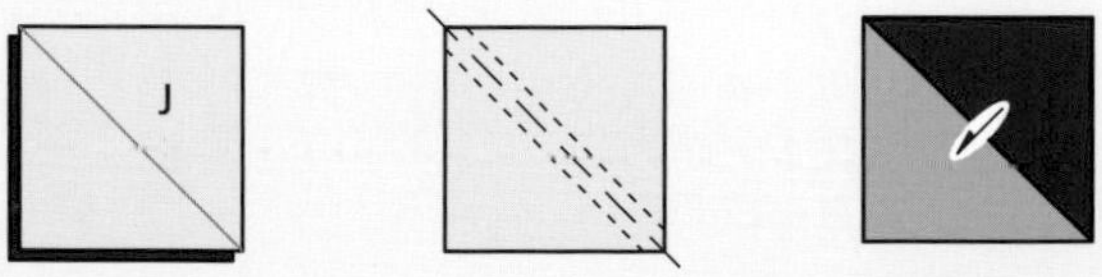

Make 24.

2. Sew white A triangles to adjacent sides of a green D square. Make 20. Then sew violet J triangles to the diagonal edges of 12 of the units.

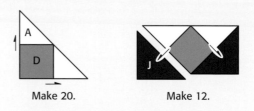

Make 20.   Make 12.

3. Sew triangle squares made in step 1 to opposite ends of the rectangular units made in step 2 to make section 1. Make 12.

Section 1.
Make 12.

4. Sew a red A triangle to the top edge of a violet F parallelogram. Make eight of each mirror image.

Make 8 of each.

5. Sew yellow B triangles to adjacent edges of a violet C square. Make 20. Sew a violet J triangle to four of the pieced triangles to make corners.

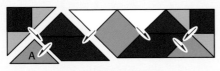

Make 20. Corner.
Make 4.

6. Sew the units made in step 4 to adjacent sides of a white/green unit made in step 2. Sew orange A triangles to the diagonal edges of the violet parallelograms. Then sew the yellow/violet pieced triangles made in step 5 to each remaining corner. Make eight section 2 units.

Section 2.
Make 8.

7. Sew three section 1 units and two section 2 units together, alternating them as shown. Make four. Sew a pieced corner made in step 5 to both ends of two of the pieced borders.

Top/bottom border.
Make 2.

Side border.
Make 2.

8. Sew the pieced borders without corners to the top and bottom edges of the quilt. Sew the pieced borders with corners onto the sides.

9. Referring to "Mitered Corners" on page 14, match center points, pin the 2" violet strips to the 4¼" animal print strips, and sew them together. Matching center points, pin the joined border strips to the quilt top and sew, backstitching ¼" from the end points. Miter the corners.

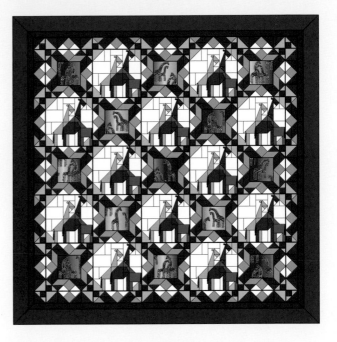

Finishing the Quilt

Referring to "Finishing the Quilt" on page 15, prepare the backing fabric and then layer the backing, batting, and quilt top. After basting the layers together, hand or machine quilt as desired. Bind your quilt using the 2¼"-wide multicolored strips.

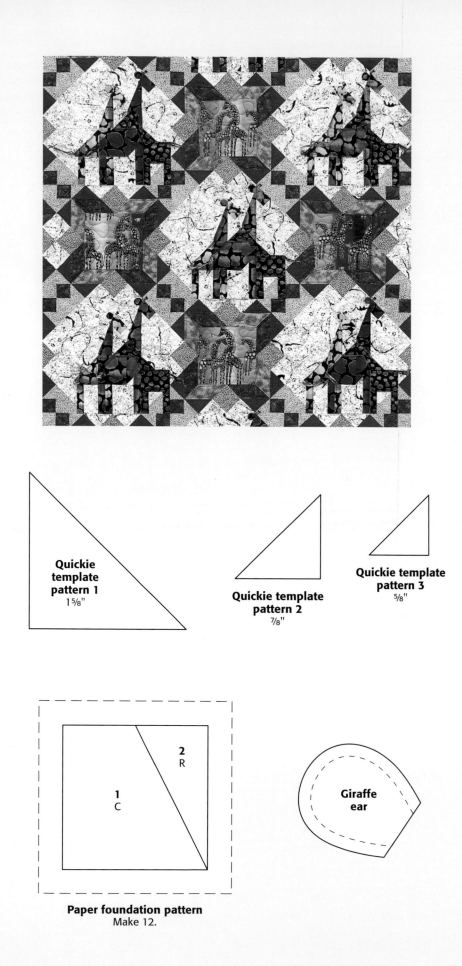

**Quickie
template
pattern 1**
1 5/8"

**Quickie template
pattern 2**
7/8"

**Quickie template
pattern 3**
5/8"

2
R

1
C

**Giraffe
ear**

Paper foundation pattern
Make 12.

Quilts with Character Prints

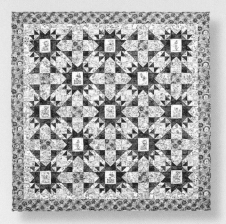

Arizona Winds

Page 62

Makin' Tracks

Page 67

Best Friend's Baskets

Page 73

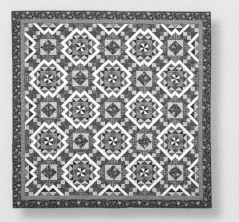

Pershing Pinwheel Stars

Page 80

Starry Lane

Page 86

Arizona Winds

Designed by Claudia Olson and made by Pat Peyton. Machine quilted by Jill Therriault.
Finished quilt: 72½" x 72½" » Finished blocks: 12"

A lovely fairy print fills the center of the Arizona blocks, while the Summer Winds blocks feature pastel colors to create a soft background for the piecing. Choose a feature print with motifs that will fit in a 4" x 5" rectangle, or the alternate 4" x 4" square in the center.

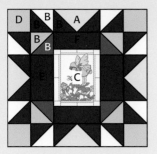

Arizona block
(rectangular center)

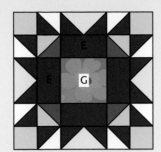

Alternate Arizona block
(square center)

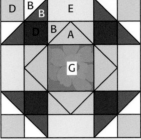

Summer Winds block

Materials

Yardage is based on 42"-wide fabric.

- 2 yards of lavender floral print for Summer Winds blocks, border, and binding*
- 1⅝ yards of rose print for blocks
- 1⅛ yards of pink print for blocks and pieced border
- 1⅛ yards of cream print for blocks and pieced border
- 1 yard of yellow print for blocks and pieced border
- ⅞ yard of light green print for blocks and pieced border
- ⅝ yard of purple print for blocks
- ⅝ yard of feature print for Arizona blocks**
- 4½ yards of fabric for backing
- 79" x 79" piece of batting

If you prefer to cut lengthwise borders, you'll need 2¼ yards.

**Extra fabric has been added for fussy cutting. Purchase this amount, or enough for 13 character repeats.*

CUTTING FOR 13 ARIZONA BLOCKS (with rectangular center)

Fabric	Piece	Number of Strips	Strip Width	Cut
Cream	B	4	2⅞"	52 squares, 2⅞" x 2⅞"
Rose	B	8	2⅞"	104 squares, 2⅞" x 2⅞"
	E	2	4½"	26 rectangles, 2½" x 4½"
	F	1 and remainder of E strip	4½"	26 rectangles, 2" x 4½"
Pink	B	2	2⅞"	26 squares, 2⅞" x 2⅞"
Purple	B	2	2⅞"	26 squares, 2⅞" x 2⅞"
Light Green	D	4	2½"	52 squares, 2½" x 2½"
Yellow	A	2	5¼"	13 squares, 5¼" x 5¼"
Feature Fabric	C	2*	4½"	13 rectangles, 4½" x 5½"

CUTTING FOR 13 ALTERNATE ARIZONA BLOCKS (with square center)

Cutting is the same as above, but *don't* cut the C or F pieces. Instead, cut the following:				
Feature Fabric	G	2*	4½"	13 squares, 4½" x 4½"
Rose	E	2	4½"	26 rectangles, 2½" x 4½" (for a total of 52)
Don't cut strips if you plan to fussy cut your pieces.				

Piecing the Arizona Blocks

1. Referring to "Half-Square Triangles" on page 10, layer a cream B square on a rose B square. Stitch, cut, and press. Sew 52 to make 104 triangle squares. Repeat with a pink B square on a purple B square. Sew 26 to make 52 triangle squares.

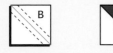

Make 104.   Make 52.

2. Sew a cream/rose triangle square to a light green D square as shown. Then sew a cream/rose triangle square to a pink/purple triangle square as shown. Make 52 of each. Sew the units together to make a four-patch unit. Make 52.

Make 52.

3. Referring to "Flying-Geese Units" on page 12, position rose B squares on opposite corners of a yellow A square. Draw, stitch, cut, and press. Make 13. Position a rose B square on the remaining yellow corners. Stitch, cut, and press to make 52 flying-geese units.

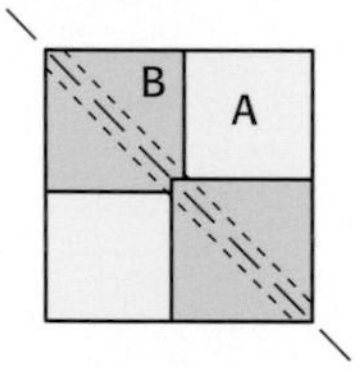

Make 52.

4. Sew a flying-geese unit to a rose E rectangle as shown. Then sew a flying-geese unit to a rose F rectangle. Make 26 of each. (For square centers, sew all flying-geese units to a rose E rectangle.)

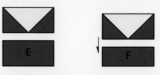

Make 26 of each.

5. Lay out the pieced units along with a feature fabric C rectangle (or a feature fabric G square if making square centers). Sew the units together into rows.

6. Join the rows to complete an Arizona block. Make 13.

Make 13.

CUTTING FOR 12 SUMMER WINDS BLOCKS

Fabric	Piece	Number of Strips	Strip Width	Cut
Cream	B	4	2⅞"	48 squares, 2⅞" x 2⅞"
Purple	B	4	2⅞"	48 squares, 2⅞" x 2⅞"
Pink	A	2	5¼"	12 squares, 5¼" x 5¼"
	D	3	2½"	48 squares, 2½" x 2½"
Rose	D	3	2½"	48 squares, 2½" x 2½"
Light Green	B	4	2⅞"	48 squares, 2⅞" x 2⅞"
Yellow	E	3	4½"	48 rectangles, 2½" x 4½"
Lavender Floral	G	2	4½"	12 squares, 4½" x 4½"

Piecing the Summer Winds Blocks

1. Use the half-square-triangle technique. Position a cream B square on a purple B square. Stitch, cut, and press. Sew 48 to create 96 triangle squares.

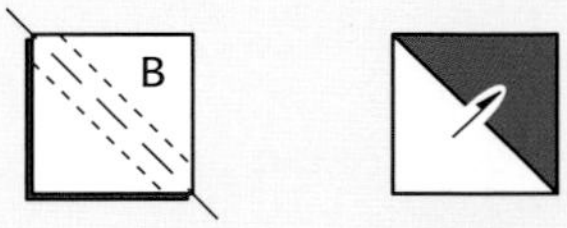

Make 96.

2. Sew a pink D square to a triangle square made in step 1. Repeat to sew a rose D square to a triangle square as shown. Make 48 of each. Sew the units together to make a four-patch unit. Make 48.

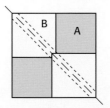

Make 48.

3. Using the flying-geese technique, place light green B squares on opposite corners of a pink A square. Draw, stitch, cut, and press. Make 12. Place green B squares on the remaining pink corners. Stitch, cut, and press to make 48 flying-geese units.

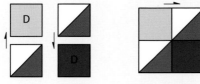

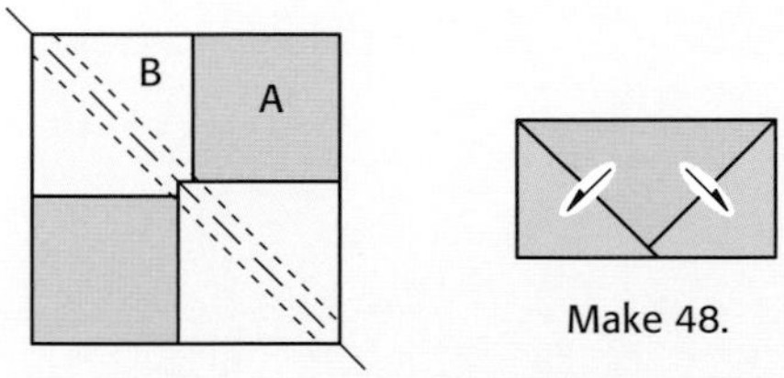

Make 48.

4. Sew yellow E rectangles to the flying-geese units. Make 48.

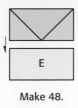

Make 48.

5. Lay out and sew together the pieced units and the lavender floral G squares in rows.

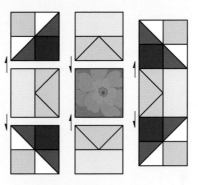

6. Join the rows to complete a Summer Winds block. Make 12.

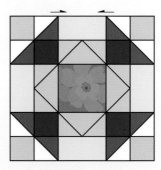

Make 12.

CUTTING FOR BORDERS AND BINDING

Fabric	Piece	Number of Strips	Strip Width	Cut
Cream	B	1	2⅞"	12 squares, 2⅞" x 2⅞"
	D	1	2½"	16 squares, 2½" x 2½"
	E	1	4½"	12 rectangles, 2½" x 4½"
Pink	B	2	2⅞"	20 squares, 2⅞" x 2⅞"
	D	2	2½"	24 squares, 2½" x 2½"
Yellow	A	1	5¼"	2 squares, 5¼" x 5¼"
Light Green	D	2	2½"	20 squares, 2½" x 2½"
Lavender Floral	Border	8	4½"	
	Binding	8	2¼"	

Piecing the Borders

1. Use the half-square-triangle method. Position a cream B square on a pink B square. Stitch, cut, and press. Sew 12 to make 24 triangle squares.

Make 24.

2. Sew the triangle squares made in step 1 to opposite ends of a cream E rectangle. Make 12.

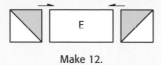

Make 12.

3. Sew a pink D square to each end of the unit made in step 2 to make a section 1 unit. Make 12.

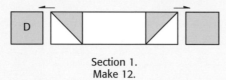

Section 1.
Make 12.

4. Using the flying-geese technique, position pink B squares on a yellow A square. Stitch, cut, and press. Use two A squares to make eight flying-geese units.

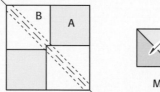

Make 8.

5. Sew a cream D square and a light green D square to both ends of the flying-geese units as shown to make a section 2 unit. Make eight.

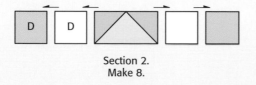

Section 2.
Make 8.

6. Sew three section 1 units and two section 2 units together, alternating them as shown to make a pieced border. Make four. Sew a light green D square to both ends of two of the pieced borders.

Make 2.

Make 2.

Assembling the Quilt Top

1. Arrange the blocks in five rows of five blocks each, alternating the blocks as shown.

2. Sew the two pieced borders without green squares to opposite sides of the quilt top.

3. Sew the two borders with green squares to the top and bottom edges of the quilt.

4. Referring to "Mitered Corners" on page 14, make four lavender floral border strips that measure 4½" x 75". Match centers, pin, and sew the border strips to all four sides of the quilt top. Miter the corners.

Finishing the Quilt

Referring to "Finishing the Quilt" on page 15, prepare the backing fabric and then layer the backing, batting, and quilt top. After basting the layers together, hand or machine quilt as desired. Bind your quilt using the 2¼"-wide lavender floral strips.

Makin' Tracks

Designed by Claudia Olson and made by Trudee Barritt. Machine quilted by Jill Therriault.
Finished quilt: 70½" x 70½" » Finished blocks: 10"

The center of the Hill and Crag block is perfect for showcasing a fun character print like this one, which features dogs driving cars. Use your character fabric in the border of this quilt to tie in the colors and theme. The alternate Goose Tracks block adds diagonal movement.

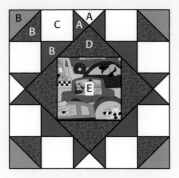

Hill and Crag block

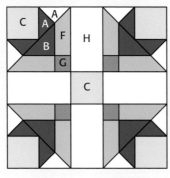

Goose Tracks block

Materials

Yardage is based on 42"-wide fabric.

- 2⅝ yards of royal blue print for blocks, border, and binding*
- 2 yards of white print for blocks and pieced border
- 2 yards of character print for Hill and Crag blocks and border**
- ¾ yard of light blue print for Goose Tracks blocks and pieced border
- ¾ yard of purple print for Hill and Crag blocks and pieced border
- ⅝ yard of yellow print for Goose Tracks blocks and pieced border
- ⅝ yard of pink print for blocks and pieced border
- 4⅜ yards of fabric for backing
- 77" x 77" piece of batting

Includes enough yardage for borders to be cut lengthwise or crosswise.

**If your print is directional or if you prefer to cut lengthwise borders, you'll need 2¾ yards; 2 yards includes extra for fussy cutting.*

CUTTING FOR 13 HILL AND CRAG BLOCKS

Fabric	Piece	Number of Strips	Strip Width	First Cut	Second Cut
Pink	B	2	2⅞"	26 squares, 2⅞" x 2⅞"	
Purple	B	2	2⅞"	26 squares, 2⅞" x 2⅞"	
	D	2	5¼"	13 squares, 5¼" x 5¼"	Cut all squares ⊠
White	A	2	3¼"	13 squares, 3¼" x 3¼"	
	C	7	2½"	104 squares, 2½" x 2½"	
Royal Blue	A	3	3¼"	26 squares, 3¼" x 3¼"	Cut 13 squares ⊠
	B	2	2⅞"	26 squares, 2⅞" x 2⅞"	Cut all squares ◹
Character Print	E	2*	4½"	13 squares, 4½" x 4½"	

Don't cut strips if you plan to fussy cut your pieces.

Piecing the Hill and Crag Blocks

1. Referring to "Half-Square Triangles" on page 10, place a pink B square on a purple B square. Stitch, cut, and press. Sew 26 to make 52 triangle squares.

Make 52.

2. Repeat with a white A square on a royal blue A square. Stitch, cut, and press. Sew 13 to make 26 triangle squares. Cut the triangle squares in half diagonally in the direction opposite the seam to make 52 triangle pairs.

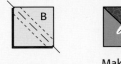

Make 26.   Cut to make 52.

3. Sew the pink/purple triangle squares made in step 1 to white C squares as shown. Then sew a white C square to a royal blue B triangle. Sew the units together to make four-patch units that appear to be missing a corner. Make 52.

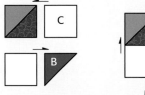

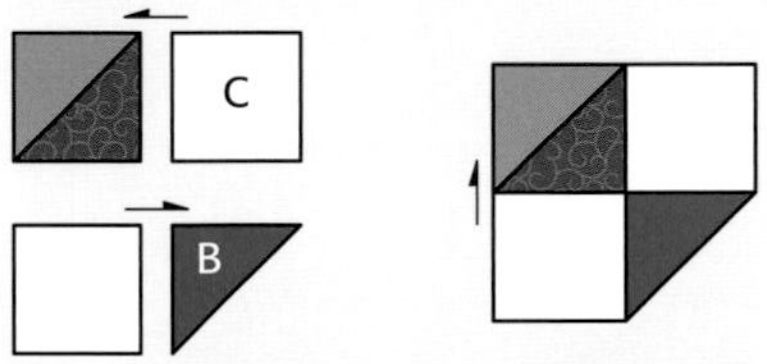

Make 52.

4. Sew royal blue A triangles to opposite ends of one unit made in step 3 as shown to make unit A. Make 26. Sew mirror-image triangle units made in step 2 to opposite ends of the remaining units from step 3 as shown to make unit B. Position the white triangles facing out. Make 26.

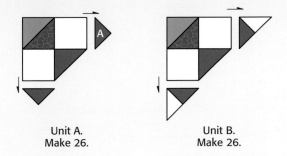

Unit A.   Unit B.
Make 26.   Make 26.

5. Sew purple D triangles to each side of a character print E square to make a center square. Make 13.

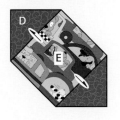 

Make 13.

6. Sew unit A pieces to opposite sides of a center square. Sew unit B pieces to the remaining sides of the center square to complete the Hill and Crag block. Make 13.

Make 13.

CUTTING FOR 12 GOOSE TRACKS BLOCKS

Fabric	Piece	Number of Strips	Strip Width	First Cut	Second Cut
White	A	2	3¼"	24 squares, 3¼" x 3¼"	
	H	3	4½"	48 rectangles, 2½" x 4½"	
Royal Blue	A	2	3¼"	24 squares, 3¼" x 3¼"	
	B	2	2⅞"	24 squares, 2⅞" x 2⅞"	Cut all squares ◻
Yellow	C	4	2½"	60 squares, 2½" x 2½"	
Pink	G	2	1½"	Leave strips uncut.	
Light Blue	F	4	3½"	48 rectangles, 1½" x 3½"; leave 2 strips uncut.	

Piecing the Goose Tracks Blocks

1. Using the half-square-triangle technique, place a white A square on a royal blue A square. Stitch, cut, and press. Sew 24 to make 48 triangle squares. Cut the triangle squares in half diagonally to make 96 triangle pairs.

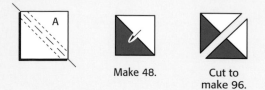

Make 48.

Cut to make 96.

2. Sew mirror-image triangle pairs to adjacent sides of a yellow C square as shown. Position the white triangles on the outside. Make 48.

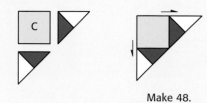

Make 48.

3. Sew a pink G strip to a light blue F strip. Make two strip sets. Cut 48 segments, 1½" x 4½", from the strip sets.

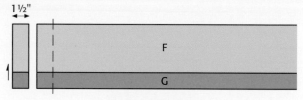

Make 2 strip sets.
Cut 48 segments.

4. Sew a royal blue B triangle to the left of a light blue F rectangle as shown. Sew a pink/light blue segment made in step 3 to the bottom of the royal blue B triangle. Line up a rotary ruler with the diagonal edge of the B triangle and trim the corners off the light blue rectangles. Make 48.

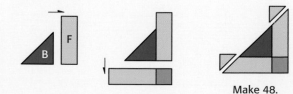

Make 48.

5. Sew the triangle unit made in step 2 to the triangle unit made in step 4 to make a flower square. Make 48. Sew a white H rectangle between two flower squares. Make 24.

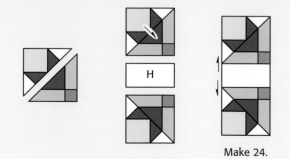

Make 24.

6. Sew white H rectangles to opposite sides of a yellow C square to make a center strip. Make 12. Lay out and sew a flower unit from step 5 to each side of the center strip to complete a Goose Tracks block. Make 12.

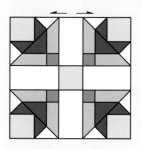

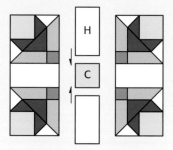

Make 12.

CUTTING FOR BORDERS AND BINDING

Fabric	Piece	Number of Strips	Strip Width	First Cut	Second Cut
Royal Blue	A	1	3¼"	12 squares, 3¼" x 3¼"	
	B	2	2⅞"	22 squares, 2⅞" x 2⅞"	Cut 12 squares ◨
	Border	16	1½"		
	Binding	8	2¼"		
White	A	1	3¼"	12 squares, 3¼" x 3¼"	
	C	2	2½"	24 squares, 2½" x 2½"	
	H	2	2½"	12 rectangles, 2½" x 4½"	
	I	1 and remainder of H strip	2½"	8 rectangles, 2½" x 6½"	
Yellow	C	2	2½"	24 squares, 2½" x 2½"	
Light Blue	F	2	3½"	24 rectangles, 1½" x 3½"; leave 1 strip uncut.	
Pink	B	2	2⅞"	20 squares, 2⅞" x 2⅞"	
	G	1	1½"	Leave strip uncut.	
Purple	B	1	2⅞"	10 squares, 2⅞" x 2⅞"	
	C	1	2½"	8 squares, 2½" x 2½"	
Character Print	Border	8*	4½"		

If your character print is directional, cut four 4½" x 42" crosswise strips and two 4½" x 76" lengthwise strips. Piece the crosswise strips to make two strips, each 76" in length.

Piecing the Borders

1. Referring to steps 1–5 of "Piecing the Goose Tracks Blocks" on page 70, make 12 joined flower units. These will be section 1 units.

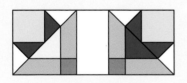

Section 1.
Make 12.

2. Use the half-square triangle technique to position a pink B square on a purple B square. Stitch, cut, and press. Repeat with a pink B square on a royal blue B square. Sew 10 of each to make 20 triangle squares of each color combination.

Make 20 of each.

3. Sew pink/purple triangle squares made in step 2 to opposite ends of a white I rectangle as shown. Make eight.

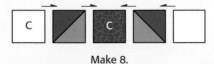

Make 8.

4. Sew pink/royal blue triangle squares made in step 2 to opposite sides of a purple C square as shown. Then sew white C squares to each end. Make eight.

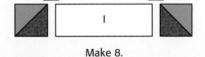

Make 8.

5. Sew the unit made in step 3 to the unit made in step 4 as shown to make a section 2 unit. Make eight.

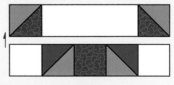

Section 2.
Make 8.

6. Sew the remaining pink/purple triangle squares made in step 2 to white C squares. Repeat to sew pink/royal blue triangle squares to white C squares. Sew the two units together to make four-patch units for the corners. Make four.

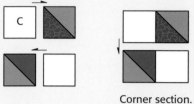

Corner section.
Make 4.

7. Sew three section 1 units to two section 2 units, alternating them as shown to make a pieced border. Make four. Sew the corner squares to both ends of two of the pieced borders.

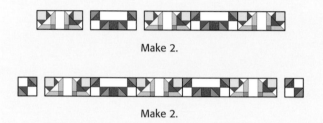

Make 2.

Make 2.

Assembling the Quilt Top

1. Arrange the blocks in five rows of five blocks each, alternating them as shown in the quilt diagram. Join the rows.

2. Sew the pieced borders without corner squares to opposite sides of the quilt. Then sew the pieced borders with corner squares to the top and bottom edges of the quilt.

3. Referring to "Mitered Corners" on page 14, make four royal blue strips that measure 1½" x 66", and four strips that measure 1½" x 76". Matching center points, pin and sew the 1½" x 66" royal blue strips to the inside edge of the 4½" x 76" character print strips; then sew the 1½" x 76" royal blue strips to the outside edge. Matching centers, pin and sew the joined strips to the quilt top and miter the corners.

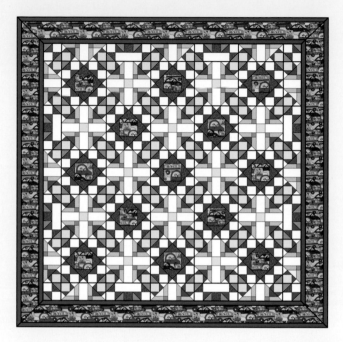

Finishing the Quilt

Referring to "Finishing the Quilt" on page 15, prepare the backing fabric and then layer the backing, batting, and quilt top. After basting the layers together, hand or machine quilt as desired. Bind your quilt using the 2¼"-wide royal blue strips.

Best Friend's Baskets

Designed and made by Claudia Olson. Machine quilted by Jill Therriault.
Finished quilt: 66" x 66" » Finished blocks: 14"

I altered the Best Friend block to accommodate a large-scale princess print, complete with magical frogs and wands. The lines of the corner triangles where the blocks join make a strong diagonal connection across the quilt. Choose a character print that will finish to be a 6" x 6" square for the block center.

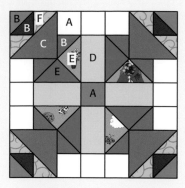

Double Flower Baskets block

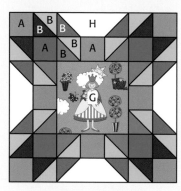

Best Friend block

Materials

Yardage is based on 42"-wide fabric.

◆ 2¼ yards of hot pink print for blocks, borders, and binding*

◆ 2 yards of character print for blocks and borders**

◆ 1⅛ yards of dark green print for blocks and pieced border

◆ 1 yard of white print for blocks and pieced border

◆ ⅝ yard of orange print for blocks and pieced border

◆ ⅝ yard of yellow print for Best Friend blocks and pieced border

◆ ⅝ yard of medium pink print for Best Friend blocks and pieced border

◆ ⅝ yard of turquoise print for blocks and pieced border

◆ ⅜ yard of yellow swirl for Double Flower Baskets blocks and pieced border

◆ ⅜ yard of light pink print for Double Flower Baskets blocks and pieced border

◆ 4 yards of fabric for backing

◆ 72" x 72" piece of batting

Includes enough yardage for border to be cut lengthwise or crosswise.

**Includes enough yardage for fussy cutting and for border to be cut lengthwise or crosswise.*

CUTTING FOR 4 DOUBLE FLOWER BASKETS BLOCKS

Fabric	Piece	Number of Strips	Strip Width	First Cut	Second Cut
Orange	B	1	2⅞"	8 squares, 2⅞" x 2⅞"	
	A	Remainder of B strip	2½"	4 squares, 2½" x 2½"	
Hot Pink	B	1	2⅞"	8 squares, 2⅞" x 2⅞"	
Yellow Swirl	F	1	3½"	16 rectangles, 2½" x 3½"	
Dark Green	B	2	2⅞"	16 squares, 2⅞" x 2⅞"	Cut all squares ◹
	C	1	5½"	8 rectangles, 4½" x 5½"	
Character Print	E	1	5¼"	4 squares, 5¼" x 5¼"	
Turquoise	E	1	5¼"	4 squares, 5¼" x 5¼"	
White	A	3	2½"	48 squares, 2½" x 2½"	
Light Pink	D	1	4½"	16 rectangles, 2½" x 4½"	

Piecing the Double Flower Baskets Blocks

1. Referring to "Half-Square Triangles" on page 10, position an orange B square on a hot pink B square. Stitch, cut, and press. Sew eight to create 16 triangle squares.

Make 16.

2. Referring to "Triangle-Trio Squares" on page 11, sew a yellow swirl F rectangle to the hot pink side of the triangle squares made in step 1. Make 16. Sew two units together and press the seams in opposite directions. Make a 4½" triangle template (pattern on page 79) and draw diagonal lines on the wrong side of the unit. Sew the unit to a dark green C rectangle, sewing on each drawn line. Cut between the drawn lines, press, and trim the resulting units to be 4½" squares. Sew eight to create 16 triangle-trio units.

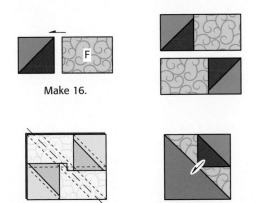

Make 16.

Make 16.

3. Referring to "Quarter-Square Triangles" on page 10, place a character print E square on a turquoise E square. Draw, sew to the right of the drawn lines, cut, and press. Sew four to create 16 triangle pairs.

Make 16.

4. Sew a dark green B triangle to a white A square. Make 16 of each mirror image.

Make 16 of each.

5. Sew the mirror-image units to each green side of the unit made in step 2. Make 16. Sew the triangle pairs made in step 3 to the diagonal edge of the units just made to make a double basket. Make 16.

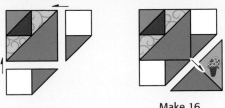

Make 16.

6. Sew a white A square to a light pink D rectangle. Make 16.

Make 16.

7. Sew a pieced rectangle made in step 6 between two double baskets made in step 5, keeping the white squares side by side. Make eight.

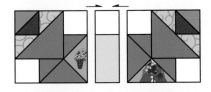

8. Sew pieced rectangles made in step 6 to opposite sides of an orange A square. Make four. Sew these units between the double basket units to complete the Double Flower Baskets block. Make four.

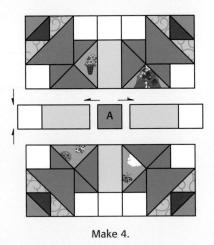

Make 4.

CUTTING FOR 5 BEST FRIEND BLOCKS

Fabric	Piece	Number of Strips	Strip Width	Cut
Yellow	B	4	2⅞"	40 squares, 2⅞" x 2⅞"
Hot Pink	B	2	2⅞"	20 squares, 2⅞" x 2⅞"
Orange	B	2	2⅞"	20 squares, 2⅞" x 2⅞"
Medium Pink	A	3	2½"	40 squares, 2½" x 2½"
Turquoise	A	2	2½"	20 squares, 2½" x 2½"
Dark Green	A	3	2½"	40 squares, 2½" x 2½"
White	H	4	2½"	20 rectangles, 2½" x 6½"
Character Print	G	1*	6½"	5 squares, 6½" x 6½"

Don't cut strips if you plan to fussy cut your pieces.

Piecing the Best Friend Blocks

1. Using the half-square-triangle method, sew a yellow B square to a hot pink B square. Stitch, cut, and press. Repeat with a yellow B square on an orange B square. Sew 20 of each to make 40 triangle squares of each combination.

Make 40 of each.

2. Sew orange/yellow triangle squares to opposite sides of a medium pink A square. Make 20.

Make 20.

3. Sew a hot pink/yellow triangle square to a medium pink A square; then sew a hot pink/yellow triangle square to a turquoise A square. Sew pairs together to make a four-patch corner unit as shown. Wait to press the last seam until you are ready to join it to the next piece. Make 20.

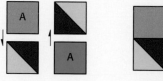

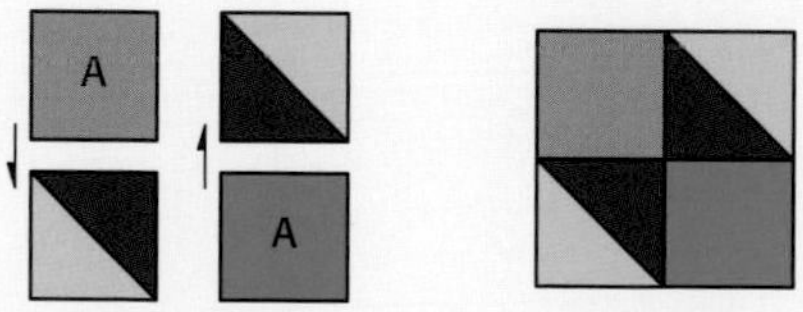

Make 20.

4. Referring to "Quick Corner Triangles" on page 11, place a dark green A square on one corner of a white H rectangle. Draw, stitch, press, and trim. Repeat to sew a dark green A square to a second corner. Make 20.

Make 20.

5. Sew the green-cornered rectangle made in step 4 to the top of the unit made in step 2. Make 20.

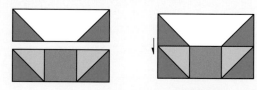

Make 20.

6. Sew units made in step 5 to the top and bottom edges of the character print G square. Make five. Sew four-patch corner units to each end of the remaining units made in step 5. Make 10. Sew these to the sides of the center square unit as shown to complete the Best Friend block. Make five.

Make 5.

CUTTING FOR BORDERS AND BINDING

Fabric	Piece	Number of Strips	Strip Width	First Cut	Second Cut
Orange	B	2	2⅞"	20 squares, 2⅞" x 2⅞"	
Hot Pink	B	2	2⅞"	20 squares, 2⅞" x 2⅞"	
	Border	8	4¼"		
	Binding	7	2¼"		
Yellow Swirl	F	1	3½"	16 rectangles, 2½" x 3½"	
Character Print	E	1	5¼"	4 squares, 5¼" x 5¼"	
	Border	7*	2½"		
Turquoise	A	1	2½"	12 squares, 2½" x 2½"	
	E	1	5¼"	4 squares, 5¼" x 5¼"	
Dark Green	A	1	2½"	8 squares, 2½" x 2½"	
	B	2	2⅞"	24 squares, 2⅞" x 2⅞"	Cut 16 squares ⬚
	C	1	5½"	8 rectangles, 4½" x 5½"	
White	A	3	2½"	40 squares, 2½" x 2½"	
	B	1	2⅞"	8 squares, 2⅞" x 2⅞"	
	H	1	2½"	4 rectangles, 2½" x 6½"	
Light Pink	D	1	2½"	8 rectangles, 2½" x 4½"	
Yellow	B	2	2⅞"	24 squares, 2⅞" x 2⅞"	
Medium Pink	A	2	2½"	20 squares, 2½" x 2½"	
	H	1	2½"	4 rectangles, 2½" x 6½"	

*If your character print is directional, cut four 2½" x 42" crosswise strips and two 2½" x 62" lengthwise strips.
Piece the crosswise strips to make two strips, each 62" in length.

Piecing the Borders

1. Follow steps 1–7 of "Piecing the Double Flower Baskets Blocks" on page 75, making a total of 16 double basket pairs. Note that in step 6, you will need to make only eight white and light pink units. You will complete eight section 1 units.

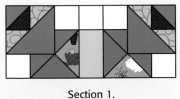

Section 1.
Make 8.

2. Using the half-square-triangle technique, layer and sew eight white and dark green, 12 yellow and orange, and 12 hot pink and yellow B squares. Join the white/green triangle squares to the yellow/orange triangle squares. Make eight of each mirror image (left-facing and right-facing pairs).

Make 16. Make 24. Make 24.

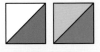

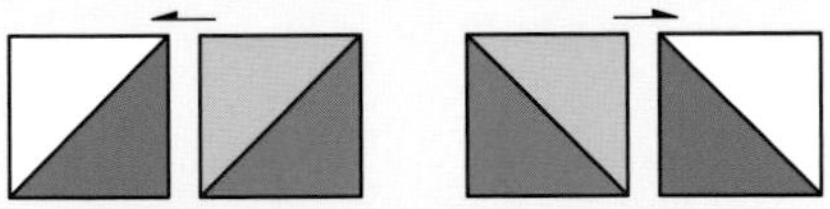

Make 8 left-facing pairs. Make 8 right-facing pairs.

3. Repeat step 3 of "Piecing the Best Friend Blocks" on page 76 to make 12 four-patch corners.

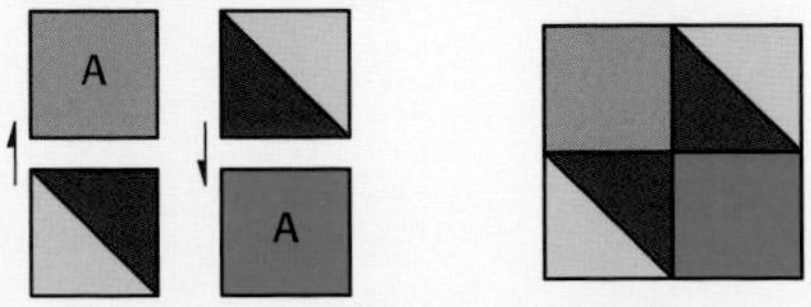

Make 12.

4. Sew the mirror-image triangle pairs made in step 2 to the top edge of the four-patch corners made in step 3. Make four of each.

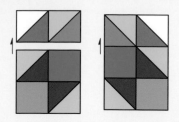

Make 4 of each.

5. Repeat steps 2, 4, and 5 of "Piecing the Best Friend Blocks" on page 76. Sew a medium pink H rectangle to the orange/pink edge of the unit as shown. Make four.

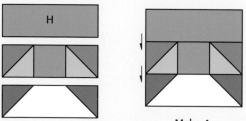

Make 4.

6. Sew the mirror-image units made in step 4 to opposite ends of the unit made in step 5 as shown to make a section 2 unit. Make four.

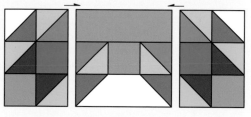

Section 2.
Make 4.

7. Sew a left-facing triangle-square pair made in step 2 to the top edge of a four-patch corner made in step 3 as shown. Then sew a medium pink A square to the orange end of the remaining four right-facing triangle-square pairs. Join the two units to make a complete corner. Make four.

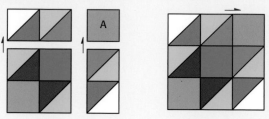

Corner unit.
Make 4.

8. Sew section 1 units to each end of a section 2 unit to make a pieced border. Make four. Sew a corner unit to both ends of two of the pieced borders.

Make 2.

Make 2.

Assembling the Quilt Top

1. Sew the blocks together into three rows of three blocks each, alternating them as shown in the quilt diagram.

2. Sew a pieced border without corners to the top and bottom edges of the quilt. Then sew a pieced border with corners to each remaining side.

3. Referring to "Mitered Corners" on page 14, make four character print borders that measure 2½" x 62". Make four hot pink borders that measure 4¼" x 70". Mark the centers of the border strips, pin, and sew them together. Then sew them to the quilt, mitering the corners.

Finishing the Quilt

Referring to "Finishing the Quilt" on page 15, prepare the backing fabric and then layer the backing, batting, and quilt top. After basting the layers together, hand or machine quilt as desired. Bind your quilt using the 2¼"-wide hot pink strips.

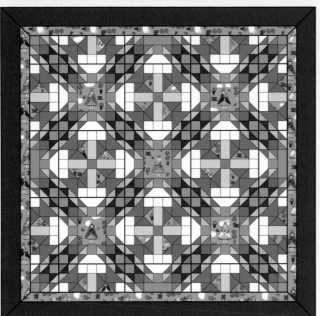

**4½" marking pattern
for triangle-trio unit**

Pershing Pinwheel Stars

Designed by Claudia Olson and made by Dianne Gillin. Machine quilted by Lynn Pittsinger.
Finished quilt: 75½" x 75½" » Finished blocks: 12"

The sunny colors in this quilt will brighten any child's room. The star points of the Pershing Pinwheel blocks are dark and surrounded by white patches to highlight them. The Jeweled Star blocks become supporting blocks. I suggest using a subtle feature fabric for the Jeweled Star block centers and border of this quilt.

Pershing Pinwheel block

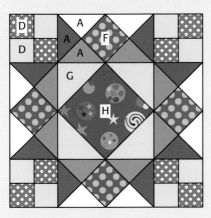

Jeweled Star block

Materials

Yardage is based on 42"-wide fabric.

- 2 yards of orange print for blocks, pieced border, and binding
- 1⅞ yards of white print for blocks and pieced border
- 1¾ yards of yellow print for blocks and pieced border
- 1½ yards of feature fabric for Jeweled Star blocks and border*
- 1⅛ yards of lime green print for Pershing Pinwheel blocks and borders*
- 1⅛ yards of hot pink print for blocks and pieced border
- 1 yard of medium purple print for blocks and pieced border
- ⅝ yard of dark purple print for Pershing Pinwheel blocks and border
- ½ yard of medium green print for Jeweled Star blocks and pieced border
- 4⅝ yards of fabric for backing
- 82" x 82" piece of batting

If you prefer to cut lengthwise borders, you'll need 2½ yards of feature fabric and 2¼ yards of lime green print.

CUTTING FOR 12 PERSHING PINWHEEL BLOCKS

Fabric	Piece	Number of Strips	Strip Width	First Cut	Second Cut
White	A	2	4¼"	12 squares, 4¼" x 4¼"	Cut all squares ⊠
	B	5	2⅜"	72 squares, 2⅜" x 2⅜"	Cut 48 squares ◺
	C	3	3⅞"	24 squares, 3⅞" x 3⅞"	
Orange	A	2	4¼"	12 squares, 4¼" x 4¼"	Cut all squares ⊠
	C	3	3⅞"	24 squares, 3⅞" x 3⅞"	
Yellow	D	3	2"	48 squares, 2" x 2"	
	E	4	3"	48 squares, 3" x 3"	
Medium Purple	E	4	3"	48 squares, 3" x 3"	
Dark Purple	B	5	2⅜"	72 squares, 2⅜" x 2⅜"	Cut 48 squares ◺
Hot Pink	A	2	4¼"	12 squares, 4¼" x 4¼"	Cut all squares ⊠
Lime Green	C	3	3⅞"	24 squares, 3⅞" x 3⅞"	Cut all squares ◺

Piecing the Pershing Pinwheel Blocks

1. Referring to "Half-Square Triangles" on page 10, position a white C square on an orange C square. Stitch, cut, and press. Sew 24 to make 48 triangle squares. Then, referring to "Quick Corner Triangles" on page 11, place a yellow D square on the corner of the white triangle. Draw, sew, press, and trim. Make 48.

Make 48.

2. Repeat the half-square-triangle technique with a yellow E square on a medium purple E square. Stitch, cut, and press. Sew 48 to produce 96 triangle squares. Repeat with white B squares on dark purple B squares. Sew 24 to make 48 triangle squares.

Make 96.   Make 48.

3. Sew together four white/dark purple triangle squares made in step 2 to make a four-patch unit. Sew hot pink A triangles to each edge. Then sew lime green C triangles to each pink edge to make a center square. Make 12.

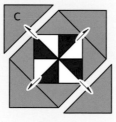

Make 12.

4. Sew a white B triangle and an orange A triangle to opposite sides of a yellow/purple triangle square made in step 2 as shown. Then sew a white A triangle and a dark purple B triangle to opposite sides of another yellow/purple triangle square as shown. Make 48 of each.

Make 48 of each.

5. Sew the units made in step 4 together. Sew a dark purple B triangle and a white B triangle to the remaining corners as shown to make a pieced rectangle. Make 48.

Make 48.

6. Sew two pieced rectangles made in step 5 to opposite sides of the center square made in step 3. Then sew a pieced rectangle between two yellow-cornered triangle squares made in step 1 as shown. Make two. Join the sections to complete a Pershing Pinwheel block. Make 12.

Make 12.

CUTTING FOR 13 JEWELED STAR BLOCKS

Fabric	Piece	Number of Strips	Strip Width	First Cut	Second Cut
Yellow	D	6	2"	Leave strips uncut.	
	G	5	3½"	52 squares, 3½" x 3½"	
Medium Purple	D	6	2"	Leave strips uncut.	
Hot Pink	A	3	4¼"	26 squares, 4¼" x 4¼"	
Orange	A	3	4¼"	26 squares, 4¼" x 4¼"	
White	A	3	4¼"	26 squares, 4¼" x 4¼"	Cut all squares ⊠
Medium Green	F	4	2⅝"	52 squares, 2⅝" x 2⅝"	
Feature Fabric	H	3	6½"	13 squares, 6½" x 6½"	

Piecing the Jeweled Star Blocks

1. Sew the yellow D strips to the medium purple D strips. Cut the joined strips into 104 segments, 2" each. Join the 2" segments to form four-patch squares. Make 52.

2"

Make 6 strip sets.
Cut 104 segments.

Make 52.

2. Using the half-square-triangle method, position a hot pink A square on an orange A square. Stitch, cut, and press. Sew 26 to make 52 triangle squares. Cut the triangle squares once diagonally as shown.

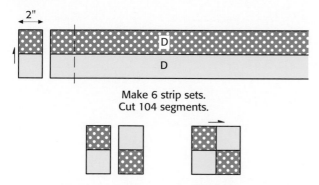

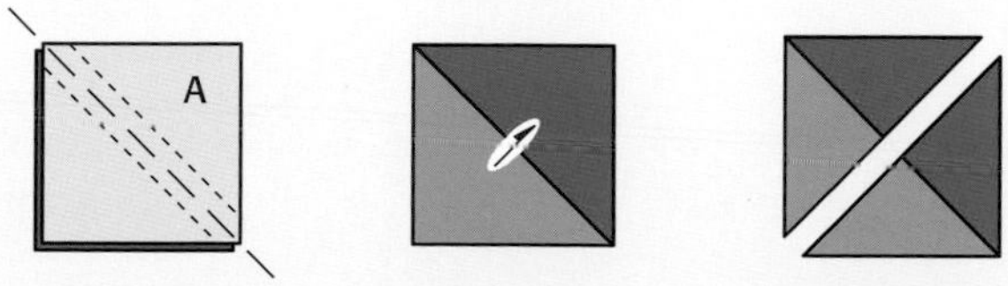

Make 52.   Cut 104.

3. Sew two white A triangles to adjacent corners of a medium green F square. Then sew the hot pink/orange triangles made in step 2 to each side as shown to make a pieced rectangle. Make 52.

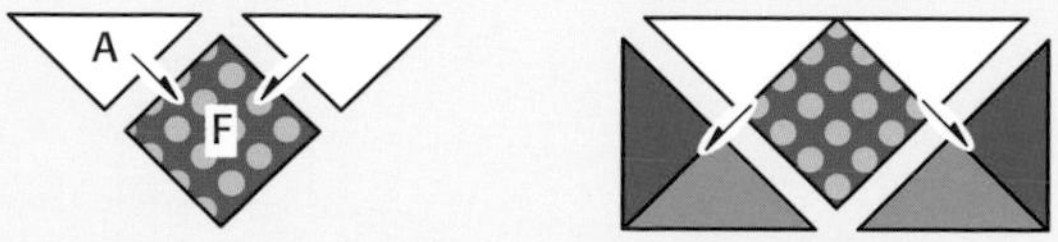

Make 52.

4. Sew a four-patch square made in step 1 to each end of the pieced rectangle just made. Make 26.

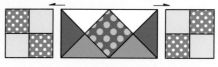

Make 26.

5. Use the quick-corner-triangle method to sew a yellow G square on the corner of a feature fabric H square. Repeat for all corners. Make 13 center squares.

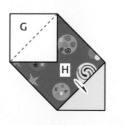
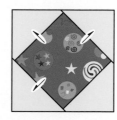

Make 13.

6. Sew pieced rectangles made in step 3 to opposite sides of the center squares. Sew the units made in step 4 to the remaining sides of this unit to complete a Jeweled Star block. Make 13.

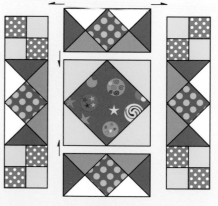

Make 13.

CUTTING FOR BORDERS AND BINDING

Fabri	Piece	Number of Strips	Strip Width	First Cut	Second Cut
White	A	1	4¼"	7 squares, 4¼" x 4¼"	Cut all squares ⊠
	B	1	2⅜"	12 squares, 2⅜" x 2⅜"	Cut all squares ◺
	C	1 and remainder of A strip	3⅞"	12 squares, 3⅞" x 3⅞"	
Hot Pink	A	1	4¼"	4 squares, 4¼" x 4¼"	
	B	1	2⅜"	12 squares, 2⅜" x 2⅜"	Cut all squares ◺
	D	2	2"	24 squares, 2" x 2"	
Orange	A	1	4¼"	4 squares, 4¼" x 4¼"	
	C	1 and remainder of A strip	3⅞"	12 squares, 3⅞" x 3⅞"	
	Binding	8	2¼"		
Yellow	D	2	2"	Leave strips uncut.	
	E	1	3"	12 squares, 3" x 3"	
Dark Purple	E	1	3"	12 squares, 3" x 3"	
Medium Purple	D	2	2"	Leave strips uncut.	
Lime Green	A	1	4¼"	3 squares, 4¼" x 4¼"	Cut all squares ⊠
	Border	8	2"		
Medium Green	F	1	2⅝"	8 squares, 2⅝" x 2⅝"	
Feature Fabric	Border	8*	3½"		

If your feature fabric is directional, cut four 3½" x 42" crosswise strips and two 3½" x 80" lengthwise strips. Piece the crosswise strips to make two strips, each 80" in length.

Piecing the Borders

1. Repeat step 1 of "Piecing the Pershing Pinwheel Blocks" on page 82, but use a hot pink D square for the quick corner triangles. Make 24.

Make 24.

2. Using the half-square-triangle technique, position a yellow E square on a dark purple E square. Stitch, cut, and press. Sew 12 to produce 24 triangle squares. Sew a white B triangle and a lime green A triangle to opposite sides of 12 of the triangle squares. Then sew a white A triangle and a hot pink B triangle to opposite sides of the other 12 triangle squares.

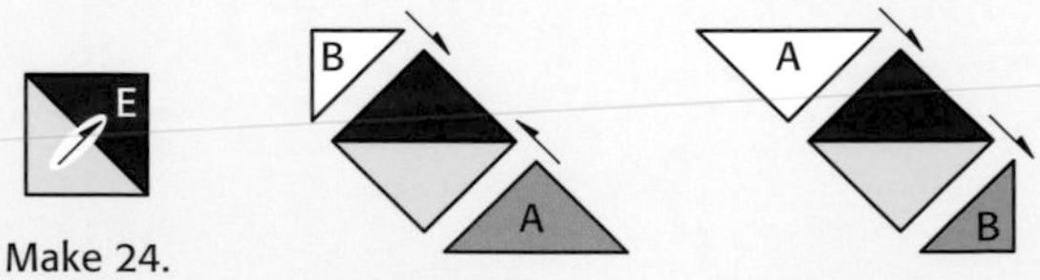

Make 24.

Make 12.   Make 12.

3. Join the units made in step 2 as shown. Sew white B triangles and hot pink B triangles to the remaining corners to make a pieced rectangle. Make 12.

Make 12.

4. Sew the pink-cornered triangle squares made in step 1 to opposite ends of the pieced rectangle made in step 3 to make border section 1. Make 12.

Section 1.
Make 12.

5. Repeat steps 1–4 of "Piecing the Jeweled Star Blocks" on page 83 to make border section 2. Make eight.

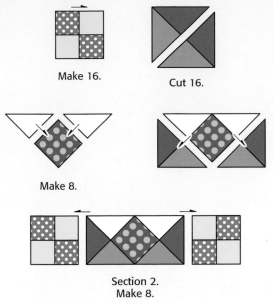

Make 16.   Cut 16.

Make 8.

Section 2.
Make 8.

6. Using the yellow/medium purple D strip set left over from step 5, make four additional four-patch units for the border corners.

Corner unit.
Make 4.

7. Sew together three border section 1 units and two border section 2 units, alternating them as shown. Repeat to make four pieced borders. Sew a corner square to opposite ends of two pieced borders.

Make 2.

Make 2.

Assembling the Quilt Top

1. Sew the Jeweled Star blocks and Pershing Pinwheel blocks in five rows of five blocks each, alternating them as shown in the quilt diagram.

2. Sew the pieced borders without corner squares to the sides of the quilt. Then sew the pieced borders with corner squares to the top and bottom edges of the quilt.

3. Referring to "Mitered Corners" on page 14, make four lime green border strips that measure 2" x 72". Make four feature fabric border strips that measure 3½" x 80". Matching centers, pin and sew the lime green strips to the feature fabric strips. Sew the border strips to the quilt and miter the corners.

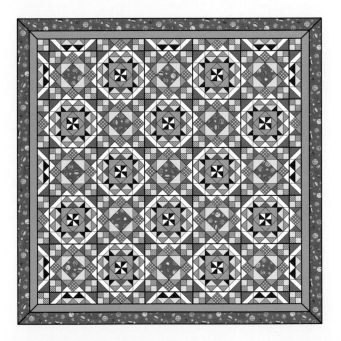

Finishing the Quilt

Referring to "Finishing the Quilt" on page 15, prepare the backing fabric and then layer the backing, batting, and quilt top. After basting the layers together, hand or machine quilt as desired. Bind your quilt using the 2¼"-wide orange strips.

Starry Lane

Designed by Claudia Olson and made by Claudia Olson and Trudee Barritt. Machine quilted by Linda Krueger.
Finished quilt: 68" x 68" » Finished blocks: 16"

Starry Lane features a border of adorable ladybug fabric. This feature fabric is also placed in the nontraditional position of star points in the Lovers' Lane blocks. The red triangles of the Lovers' Lane blocks form a strong diagonal connection between blocks. The Zigzag Eccentric Star blocks are lighter in color to fade into the background.

Zigzag Eccentric Star block

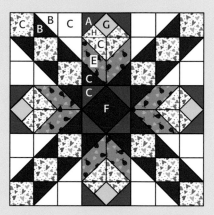

Lovers' Lane block

Materials

Yardage is based on 42"-wide fabric.

- 2¼ yards of light multicolored print for blocks and pieced border
- 2¼ yards of red print for Lovers' Lane blocks, borders, and binding*
- 1⅝ yards of feature fabric for Lovers' Lane blocks and border**
- 1⅝ yards of white print for blocks and pieced border
- ⅝ yard of purple print for blocks and pieced border
- ½ yard of hot pink print for Zigzag Eccentric Star blocks
- ⅜ yard of green print for Zigzag Eccentric Star blocks and pieced border
- ¼ yard of yellow print for Lovers' Lane blocks and pieced border
- 4¼ yards of fabric for backing
- 74" x 74" piece of batting

Includes enough yardage for border to be cut lengthwise or crosswise.

**If you prefer to cut lengthwise borders, you'll need 2¼ yards.*

CUTTING FOR 4 ZIGZAG ECCENTRIC STARS BLOCKS

Fabric	Piece	Number of Strips	Strip Width	Cut
White	B	2	2⅞"	24 squares, 2⅞" x 2⅞"
	C	1	2½"	16 squares, 2½" x 2½"
	D	1	4⅞"	8 squares, 4⅞" x 4⅞"
Purple	A	1	5¼"*	4 squares, 5¼" x 5¼"
Hot Pink	B	2	2⅞"	24 squares, 2⅞" x 2⅞"
	C	2	2½"	32 squares, 2½" x 2½"
Multicolored Print	A	1	5¼"*	4 squares, 5¼" x 5¼"
	B	3	2⅞"	32 squares, 2⅞" x 2⅞"
	C	1	2½"	16 squares, 2½" x 2½"
	D	1	4⅞"	8 squares, 4⅞" x 4⅞"
	E	1	4½"	16 rectangles, 2½" x 4½"
	F	1	4½"	4 squares, 4½" x 4½"
Green	A	1	5¼"*	4 squares, 5¼" x 5¼"
Save the remainders of the strips for the borders.				

Piecing the Zigzag Eccentric Stars Blocks

1. Referring to "Flying-Geese Units" on page 12, place white B squares on opposite corners of a purple A square. Draw, stitch, cut, and press. Repeat with hot pink B squares on a multicolored A square and with multicolored B squares on a green A square. Use four A squares of each to create 16 of each flying-geese combination.

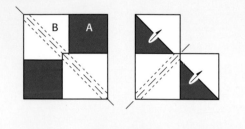

Make 16 of each.

2. Sew the flying-geese units together in groups of three as shown. Make eight of each.

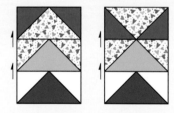

Make 8 of each.

3. Sew units made in step 2 to opposite sides of a multicolored F square, pointing the geese toward the F square. Make four.

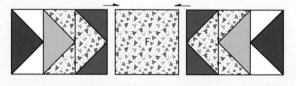

Make 4.

4. Referring to "Quick Corner Triangles" on page 11, sew a white C square on the corner of a multicolored E rectangle. Repeat and sew a hot pink C square on the adjacent corner. Make eight of each mirror-image flying-geese unit.

Make 8 of each.

5. Sew a hot pink C square to the hot pink ends of the flying-geese units just made.

Make 8 of each.

6. Referring to "Half-Square Triangles" on page 10, position a white B square on a multicolored B square. Stitch, cut, and press. Repeat to sew a multicolored B square to a hot pink B square. Sew eight of each to create 16 triangle squares of each combination. Sew the triangle squares together in pairs as shown. Make eight of each.

Make 16 of each.

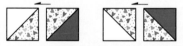

Make 8 of each.

7. Using the half-square-triangle method, position a white D square on a multicolored D square. Sew eight to make 16 triangle squares. Sew a multicolored C square to the white corner of a triangle square to make a corner triangle. Press and trim. Make 16.

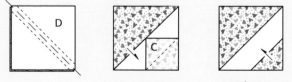

Make 16.

8. Sew the pairs of triangle squares made in step 6 to the units made in step 7 as shown. Make eight of each.

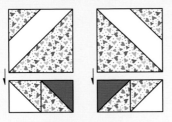

Make 8 of each.

9. Sew the flying-geese units made in step 5 to the sides of the units just made as shown. Make eight of each.

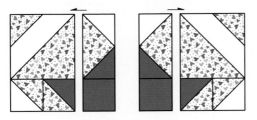

Make 8 of each.

10. Sew the mirror-image units made in step 9 to a flying-geese unit made in step 2 as shown. Make 8.

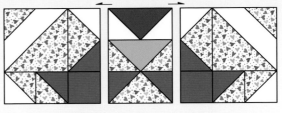

Make 8.

11. Lay out and sew two of the units made in step 10 to opposite sides of the unit made in step 3 to complete the block. Make four blocks.

Make 4.

CUTTING FOR 5 LOVERS' LANE BLOCKS

Fabric	Piece	Number of Strips	Strip Width	First Cut	Second Cut
White	B	4	2⅞"*	40 squares, 2⅞" x 2⅞"	
	C	3	2½"	40 squares, 2½" x 2½"	
Red	B	4	2⅞"*	40 squares, 2⅞" x 2⅞"	
	C	3	2½"	40 squares, 2½" x 2½"	
	F	1	4½"	5 squares, 4½" x 4½"	
Multicolored Print	C	7	2½"	100 squares, 2½" x 2½"	
	H	1	3¼"	10 squares, 3¼" x 3¼"	Cut all squares ⊠
Purple	B	2	2⅞"	20 squares, 2⅞" x 2⅞"	Cut all squares ◸
	C	1 and remainder of B strip	2½"	20 squares, 2½" x 2½"	
Feature Fabric	E	5	2½"	40 rectangles, 2½" x 4½"	
Yellow	G	1	1¹⁵⁄₁₆"	20 squares, 1¹⁵⁄₁₆" x 1¹⁵⁄₁₆"	
Save the remainders of the strips for the borders.					

Piecing the Lovers' Lane Blocks

1. Using the half-square-triangle method, position a white B square on a red B square. Stitch, cut, and press. Sew 40 to create 80 triangle squares. Sew the triangle squares to white and multicolored C squares in rows as shown. Join the rows to make a pieced square. Make 20.

Make 80.

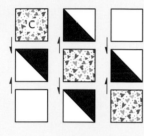

Make 20.

2. Use the quick-corner-triangle technique to sew purple C squares on the corners of a red F square as shown. Make five.

Make 5.

3. Sew a red C square on the corner of a feature fabric E rectangle; then sew a multicolored C square on the opposite corner of the feature fabric E rectangle. Make 20 of each mirror-image unit. Sew the units together.

Make 20 of each.

Make 20.

4. Sew multicolored H triangles to adjacent sides of a yellow G square. Then sew purple B triangles to each short side of the unit as shown. Make 20. Sew this unit to the top edge of the unit made in step 3 as shown. Make 20.

Make 20.

Make 20.

5. Arrange the pieced units in rows as shown. Join the rows to complete a Lovers' Lane block. Make five blocks.

Make 5.

CUTTING FOR BORDERS AND BINDING

Fabric	Piece	Number of Strips	Strip Width	First Cut	Second Cut
White	B	2 and remainder of white B strip from Lovers' Lane blocks	2⅞"	28 squares, 2⅞" x 2⅞"	
	C	1	2½"	16 squares, 2½" x 2½"	
	D	1	4⅞"	8 squares, 4⅞" x 4⅞"	
Red	B	1 and remainder of red B strip from Lovers' Lane blocks	2⅞"	16 squares, 2⅞" x 2⅞"	
	Inner border	7	1½"		
	Outer border	8	1¼"		
	Binding	8	2¼"		
Multicolored Print	A	Remainder of multi-colored A strip from Zigzag Eccentric Stars blocks	5¼"	1 square, 5¼" x 5¼"	
	B	1	2⅞"	12 squares, 2⅞" x 2⅞"	
	C	3	2½"	40 squares, 2½" x 2½"	
	D	1	4⅞"	8 squares, 4⅞" x 4⅞"	
	H	1	3¼"	2 squares, 3¼" x 3¼"	Cut all squares ⊠
Purple	A	Remainder of purple A strip from Zigzag Eccentric Stars blocks	5¼"	2 squares, 5¼" x 5¼"	
	B	1	2⅞"	8 squares, 2⅞" x 2⅞"	Cut 4 squares
Yellow	G	1	1¹⁵⁄₁₆"	4 squares, 1¹⁵⁄₁₆" x 1¹⁵⁄₁₆"	◻
Green	A	Remainder of green A strip from Zigzag Eccentric Stars blocks	5¼"	2 squares, 5¼" x 5¼"	
	E	1	4½"	16 rectangles, 2½" x 4½"	
Feature Fabric	Middle border	8*	4½"		

If your feature fabric is directional, cut four 4½" x 42" crosswise strips and two 4½" x 70" lengthwise strips. Piece the crosswise strips to make two strips, each 70" in length.

Piecing the Borders

1. Using the half-square-triangle method, place a white B square on a red B square. Stitch, cut, and press. Sew 16 to make 32 triangle squares. Repeat to sew white B squares to multicolored B squares; sew four to make eight.

Make 32.   Make 8.

2. Sew 24 of the red/white triangle squares to 24 multicolored C squares. Sew the pairs together to make four-patch units as shown. Make 12. Set four aside for the border corners.

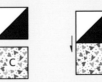

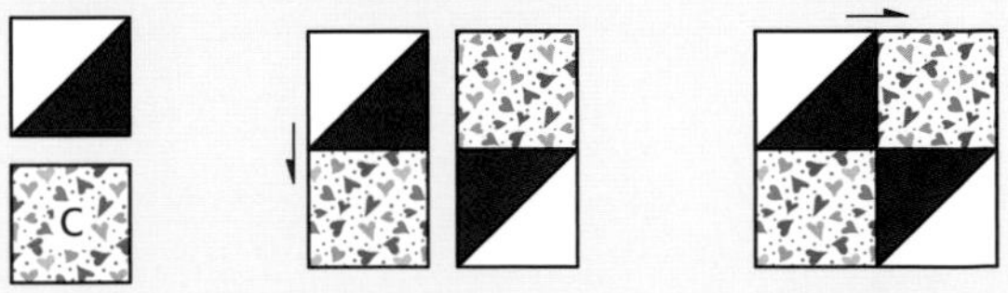

Make 12.

3. Sew the remaining eight red/white triangle squares to white/multicolored triangle squares as shown. Make four of each. Sew these to one side of the four-patch units made in step 2. Make four of each mirror image.

Make 4 of each.

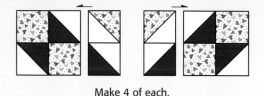

Make 4 of each.

4. Referring to "Flying-Geese Units" on page 12, place purple B squares on opposite corners of a multicolored A square. Draw, stitch, cut, and press. Use one A square to create four flying-geese units.

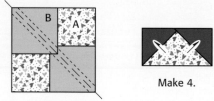

Make 4.

5. Sew multicolored H triangles to adjacent sides of a yellow G square. Then sew purple B triangles to each short side of the unit as shown. Make four. Then sew these units to the flying-geese units made in step 4.

Make 4.

6. Sew two units made in step 3 to opposite ends of a purple triangle unit made in step 5 to make a section 1 unit. Make four.

Section 1.
Make 4.

7. Using the half-square-triangle method, position a white D square on a multicolored D square. Sew eight to make 16 triangle squares. Sew a multicolored C square to the white corner of a triangle square to make a corner triangle. Press and trim. Make 16.

Make 16.

8. Using the quick-corner-triangle method, sew a white C square on one corner of a green E rectangle to make a corner triangle. Make eight of each mirror image. Sew these units to one side of the square made in step 7.

Make 8 of each.

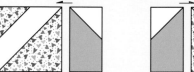

9. Using the flying-geese method, place white B squares on opposite corners of a purple A square. Draw, stitch, cut, and press. Repeat to sew multicolored B squares on a green A square. Use two A squares of each color to create eight flying-geese units of each. Join the flying-geese units in pairs. Make eight.

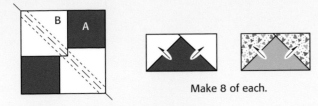

Make 8 of each.

Make 8.

10. Sew units from step 8 to each end of a flying-geese pair made in step 9 to complete a section 2 unit. Make eight.

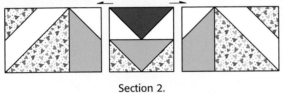

Section 2.
Make 8.

11. Sew one section 1 unit and two section 2 units together, alternating them as shown. Make four pieced borders. Sew a four-patch corner on both ends of two of the pieced borders.

Make 2.

Make 2.

Assembling the Quilt Top

1. Sew the Lovers' Lane blocks to the Zigzag Eccentric Stars blocks in three rows of three blocks each, alternating them as shown in the quilt diagram.

2. Sew two pieced borders without corner squares to opposite sides of the quilt. Sew the two pieced borders with corner squares to the top and bottom edges of the quilt.

3. Referring to "Mitered Corners" on page 14, make four red 1½" x 62" strips for the inner border and four red 1¼" x 72" strips for the outer border. Then make four feature fabric 4½" x 70" strips for the middle border. Matching the centers, sew the strips together as shown. Pin and sew the joined strips to the quilt, mitering the corners.

Make 4.

Finishing the Quilt

Referring to "Finishing the Quilt" on page15, prepare the backing fabric and then layer the backing, batting, and quilt top. After basting the layers together, hand or machine quilt as desired. Bind your quilt using the 2¼"-wide red strips.

About the Author

Claudia Olson grew up in California, but moved to Juneau, Alaska, in 1976 and then to Wenatchee, Washington, in 1991. She has a Bachelor of Arts degree and a K–12 teaching certificate from the University of California in Fullerton. She taught school for 25 years, and now does substitute teaching. For the past 12 years, she has taught quilting classes for quilt guilds and quilt shops. She is married with two grown children.

Claudia began quilting more than 18 years ago in Juneau and joined the Capital City Quilters guild. After taking a class from Marsha McCloskey, she was inspired to look at blocks and patterns in a new way to create her own unique designs. Since then, no quilt pattern has been safe from tweaking! She began to experiment with block combinations and looked for ways to make secondary patterns stand out. From there she jumped into designing quilts on the computer and developed several patterns. She enlisted help from fellow quilters in the North Central Washington Quilt Guild to make the abundance of quilts that she had designed.

This book is a follow-up to Claudia's *Two-Block Appliqué Quilts* (Martingale & Company, 2004). She likes to incorporate as many new piecing techniques into her books as possible.

Claudia enjoys teaching quilt classes, writing, designing new quilts, and traveling to meet quilters of all skill levels and especially to encourage new quilters. She can be contacted via email at twoblockquilts@yahoo.com.

New and Bestselling Titles from

Martingale® & COMPANY

America's Best-Loved Craft & Hobby Books®
America's Best-Loved Knitting Books®

 That Patchwork Place®

America's Best-Loved Quilt Books®

NEW RELEASES
Alphabet Soup
Big Knitting
Big 'n Easy
Courtship Quilts
Crazy Eights
Creating Your Perfect Quilting Space
Crochet from the Heart
Fabulous Flowers
First Crochet
Fun and Funky Crochet
Joined at the Heart
Little Box of Knitted Ponchos and Wraps, The
Little Box of Knitted Throws, The
Merry Christmas Quilts
More Crocheted Aran Sweaters
Party Time!
Perfectly Brilliant Knits
Polka-Dot Kids' Quilts
Quilt Block Bonanza
Quilts from Grandmother's Garden
Raise the Roof
Saturday Sweaters
Save the Scraps
Seeing Stars
Sensational Knitted Socks
Sensational Sashiko
Strip-Pieced Quilts
Tea in the Garden
Treasury of Scrap Quilts, A

Our books are available at bookstores and your favorite craft, fabric, and yarn retailers.
If you don't see the title you're looking for, visit us at
www.martingale-pub.com
or contact us at:
1-800-426-3126

International: 1-425-483-3313
Fax: 1-425-486-7596
Email: info@martingale-pub.com

APPLIQUÉ
Appliqué Takes Wing
Easy Appliqué Samplers
Garden Party
Stitch and Split Appliqué
Sunbonnet Sue: All through the Year
WOW! Wool-on-Wool Folk-Art Quilts

LEARNING TO QUILT
101 Fabulous Rotary-Cut Quilts
Happy Endings, Revised Edition
Loving Stitches, Revised Edition
Magic of Quiltmaking, The
Quilter's Quick Reference Guide, The
Sensational Settings, Revised Edition
Your First Quilt Book (or it should be!)

PAPER PIECING
40 Bright and Bold Paper-Pieced Blocks
50 Fabulous Paper-Pieced Stars
300 Paper-Pieced Quilt Blocks
Easy Machine Paper Piecing
Fanciful Quilts to Paper Piece
Hooked on Triangles
Quilter's Ark, A
Show Me How to Paper Piece

QUILTS FOR BABIES & CHILDREN
American Doll Quilts
Even More Quilts for Baby
More Quilts for Baby
Quilts for Baby
Sweet and Simple Baby Quilts

ROTARY CUTTING/SPEED PIECING
40 Fabulous Quick-Cut Quilts
365 Quilt Blocks a Year: Perpetual Calendar
1000 Great Quilt Blocks
Clever Quilts Encore
Endless Stars
Once More around the Block
Square Dance, Revised Edition
Stack a New Deck
Star-Studded Quilts
Strips and Strings

SCRAP QUILTS
More Nickel Quilts
Nickel Quilts
Scrap Frenzy
Successful Scrap Quilts

TOPICS IN QUILTMAKING
Basket Bonanza
Cottage-Style Quilts
Everyday Folk Art
Focus on Florals
Follow the Dots . . . to Dazzling Quilts
Log Cabin Quilts
More Biblical Quilt Blocks
Quilter's Home: Spring, The
Scatter Garden Quilts
Shortcut to Drunkard's Path, A
Strawberry Fair
Summertime Quilts
Tried and True
Warm Up to Wool

CRAFTS
Bag Boutique
Collage Cards
Creating with Paint
Painted Fabric Fun
Purely Primitive
Stamp in Color
Trashformations
Vintage Workshop, The: Gifts for All Occasions
Year of Cats…in Hats!, A

KNITTING & CROCHET
200 Knitted Blocks
365 Knitting Stitches a Year: Perpetual Calendar
Classic Crocheted Vests
Crocheted Socks!
Dazzling Knits
First Knits
Handknit Style
Knitted Throws and More for the Simply Beautiful Home
Knitting with Hand-Dyed Yarns
Little Box of Crocheted Hats and Scarves, The
Little Box of Scarves, The
Little Box of Scarves II, The
Little Box of Sweaters, The
Pleasures of Knitting, The
Pursenalities
Rainbow Knits for Kids
Sarah Dallas Knitting
Ultimate Knitted Tee, The

06/05